HIDDEN POCKETS IN KYOTO

An insider's guide to the best places to eat, drink and explore

STEVE WIDE &
MICHELLE MACKINTOSH

EXPLORE

HIDDEN POCKETS
IN KYOTO

CONTENTS

WELCOME TO KYOTO

Maido.

When we first wrote our book Kyoto Pocket Precincts, *we found ourselves at the beginning of what we can only describe as a new chapter in our lives. To extend the metaphor, we had started to write a story, and chapter by chapter we have revealed new plotlines, intense dialogue and exhilarating twists and turns. Over the years we have seen our 'little green book' in many Kyoto cafes and bookstores – it has been a true delight, we feel like we have managed to unpick the complex threads of the city and somehow got closer to the heart of what it is that makes Kyoto so very, well, Kyoto. But trying to define a city for you, dear reader, means sharing moments and places, describing beauty and capturing a fleeting essence. Kyoto is not so easy – it has to be experienced.*

Kyoto is an immersive history lesson of smells, sights, sounds and feelings. You have to navigate its ancient pathways, temples, gardens and narrow, lantern-lit alleys to reveal the city's neighbourhoods and find out what makes them belong to Kyoto alone. 'Wa' is what it means to be Japanese – a way of living that encapsulates centuries of reflection, creation and inspiration – and, to us, Kyoto is the living, breathing embodiment of 'wa'. It's a city of tradition and history, where the influence of ancient temples and shrines, with their deep spiritual roots, touches every aspect of daily life.

The seasons in Kyoto are echoed in everything from food to festivals and craft, and in the intense appreciation of leaves, flowers, moss and snow. The traditional arts thrive in the city, and creators and their craft make visitors suddenly feel inspired to work with their hands, to shape beauty, to touch history. The region even has its own dialect – where the word 'maido' (above), meaning 'hello', comes from. Kyoto has become one of our favourite cities in the world. As soon as you hit Kyoto you start to slow down, become more introspective and put yourself in the moment. Whenever we visit, we absorb just a little bit more of that Kyoto tranquility into our lives.

Surrounded by mountains, always present on the skyline, Kyoto beckons you to discover its historic treasures. There are over 2000 temples and shrines to visit, plus Zen gardens, art galleries and museums. You can partake in tea ceremonies and observe geisha culture. You can eat in restaurants in centuries-old houses, and at temples that serve vegan banquets. Along the way, you'll uncover a new Kyoto – a dynamic and evolving city taking the skills and lessons of the past and using them to forge a vibrant contemporary culture. So join us, slide off your shoes, slip on a yukata (summer robe) and get ready to take life at Kyoto pace.

ABOUT KYOTO

In Kyoto you'll find more than 2000 ancient temples and shrines, and beautiful gardens and traditional buildings lining atmospheric streets. The city's pace of life, deep sense of history, handcrafting expertise and exemplary food culture give captivating and life-changing experiences to travellers.

From 794 CE, Kyoto became the capital of Japan, replacing Nara. Initially called Heian-Kyo, various names were bestowed upon the city, including Kyo and Keishi, until Kyoto was settled upon in the 11th century. Kyoto remained the capital of Japan until as late as 1868, when the Imperial Court was transferred to Tokyo. Being an ancient capital, Kyoto has an often surprisingly violent history (given that the original name Heian-Kyo meant 'tranquility and peace capital'). Famous and bloody events like the Honnoji Incident, the Kinmon Incident and the Onin War loom large over the city's past.

Originally built upon the principles of feng shui and later improved upon with a series of grid-like streets running north and south, Kyoto was designed to be easily navigated – something that you can still feel today. The large-scale destruction of Japanese cities during World War II left Kyoto largely untouched, and many relics, buildings and gardens remain from the pre-war era. This gives Kyoto a distinct feeling of natsukashii, meaning nostalgia for 'times gone by', and it is often referred to as the place that the Japanese go to *feel* Japanese.

Kyoto University is the second biggest university in Japan, making the city a great seat of learning. The history of arts and crafts is deep, rich and still shapes Kyoto's artisan shopping and temple and gallery experiences. Kyoto is also one of Japan's most prominent regions for tea production, and tea ceremonies here are an artform. The city is known for the performing arts of Noh theatre, dance, Koto playing, and storytelling. The famed Kyoto geisha have taken performance, fashion, style and hair and make-up to an otherworldly status. The Meiji Restoration in 1868 sparked 'a new Kyoto', and as part of that, the film industry was born. In 1897, the Dento Co. showed the first cinematic projection and in 1908, director Shozo Makino shot one of Japan's first movies *The Battle of Honnoji*, in Kyoto. In the 21st century a delicate modernisation is transforming Kyoto, while being careful not to erode the layers of history.

Foodies, photographers, historians and crafters alike find Kyoto irresistible. Like us, once it gets into your soul, you'll find that being away from the city for too long creates a powerful longing in your heart.

KYOTO

Key

1 Fushimi Inari shrine
2 To-ji temple
3 Kyoto Tower
4 Nijo Castle
5 Nanzen-ji temple
6 Ginkaku-ji temple
7 Sagano Bamboo Grove
8 Kinkaku-ji temple
9 Kyoto Botanical Gardens

7

NEIGHBOURHOOD INDEX

NEIGHBOURHOOD INDEX

NEIGHBOURHOOD INDEX

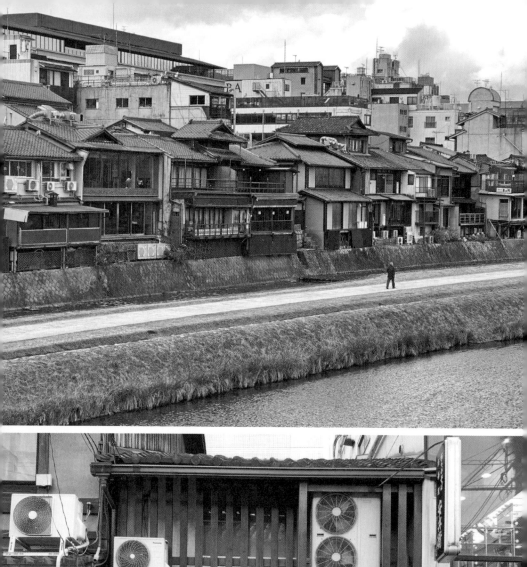

NOTABLE NEIGHBOURHOODS

*Kyoto's unmissable sights and experiences are spread across
the city in a series of areas that each manage to have their
own unique feel and their own regional history. Many,
but by no means all, of the notable temples can be found
in the north and south Higashiyama districts, while old
Kyoto's nightlife and shopping are centred around Gion and
Pontocho. Other areas embrace a contemporary Kyoto, like
the area around Kyoto Station – a symbol of a new Kyoto
that mimics the grandeur of the city's ancient temples while
forging a new future from steel and glass. Before it, Kyoto
Tower hints at a playful retro pop culture thread that runs
through Kyoto's manga and gaming culture. There is much
to discover by exploring Kyoto's neighbourhoods in detail, so
make sure you don't limit yourself to just one or two areas!*

KYOTO STATION

Kyoto's sparse southern zone is most notable for the impressive To-ji temple
(late 700s) and Kyoto Station, a cavernous structure that competes with Kyoto's
ancient temples and shrines for 'landmark' status. Chances are you'll be using the
station as more of a jumping-off point to explore Kyoto's tourist hot spots like Uji
and Nara, and the station and the area around it won't be number one on your to-
do list. But it's not just a pick-up and drop-off point. Kyoto Station is an admirable
synthesis of form and function and will amuse you for hours with a wide range of
shopping and eating opportunities, department stores, malls and even a ramen
village. South of the station, you'll find an up-and-coming neighbourhood with new
cafes, inventive hotels and vibrant local and multicultural eateries, all overseen by
the truly spectacular, towering five-storey pagoda of To-ji temple (see p. 154).

North of the station you'll find Kyoto Tower – a modernist monolith with
an observation deck that commands spectacular views of Kyoto.

NOTABLE NEIGHBOURHOODS

GOJO

Gojo-dori may seem to be an absurdly wide street bisecting the city, a conduit from Kyoto Station to bustling Shijo-dori, but if you dig a little deeper, many gems can be found hidden on and around this main thoroughfare. Beautiful examples of residential houses with artfully arranged bonsai gardens and bicycles out the front sit alongside pickle shops, boutique hotels and tiny standing bars. This understated area is where you'll find the latest designer or perfect bento box lunch. Handcraft stores are nestled in the depths of buildings, old eateries are tucked between tower blocks on the street, and new and established stores sit side by side in the alleys and lanes that trickle off the main drag. The area around Bukko-ji temple and Lantern St is home to some of the most interesting examples of artisan and concept retail stores in the city, around which a burgeoning cafe scene has emerged.

Further east, the canals offer tranquil walks and unique shopping experiences that show an enduring, diverse and, shh ... a secret side to Kyoto.

SHIJO

Get your bearings in Shijo – it's the perfect compass point for most of your Kyoto to-do list. If you thought Kyoto was all about temples and gardens, think again. Home to world-class shopping and eating, this mini city with a country atmosphere showcases the best of the best. Shijo-dori is the beating heart of the city, a busy shopping street that cuts a majestic swathe through Kyoto, but somehow manages to absorb the Zen-like calm of the mountains that overlook it. Locals and visitors flock here to shop at department stores, chic boutiques, souvenir stores and every other retail experience you can imagine.

To the east is the river, Gion and the temples of Higashiyama, to the west Nijo Castle (see p. 203) and the mountains and Sagano Bamboo Grove in Arashiyama (see p. 160), to the north the Imperial Palace Gardens and local Kyoto, and to the south Kyoto Station (see p. 137), Uji (see p. 217) and further afield, Nara (see p. 215). All around you is a panoramic view of beautiful mountains dotted with temples and shrines, basking gloriously under the impressively expansive sky. For a reprieve from shopping, stroll the peaceful grounds of Rokkaku-do (Chobo-ji) temple (see p. 163), walk the picturesque laneways in and around the canals, or head to the back streets for a plethora of tiny cafes, old-school noodle joints and Nishiki Market (see p. 63), Kyoto's unmissable foodie experience.

NOTABLE NEIGHBOURHOODS

TERAMACHI

Teramachi-dori runs north from Shijo-dori, beginning as a covered arcade that awaits crowds spilling out from the eastern end of Nishiki Market (see p. 63). Known as the 'art avenue,' it starts with a plethora of cut-price stores, a minor tourist-trap (albeit with some standout moments), before morphing into one of Kyoto's best shopping strips (see p. 117).

Once you have crossed expansive Oike-dori, Teramachi has some of Kyoto's most renowned traditional craft stores. Anyone seeking out calligraphy tools, paper, antiques, vintage textiles and fabrics, tea, lacquerware, incense and ceramics should not miss it.

PONTOCHO

Ah, the Floating World – a narrow street crammed with tiny bars and eateries and beautifully preserved townhouses where geisha and maiko (apprentice geisha) have tip-tapped between appointments in exclusive teahouses and clubs since the 1600s. This is like an Edo period (1603–1867) pleasure zone. Kabuki actors, sumo wrestlers and more than a few shady characters come here to let off steam, and there's no reason why you shouldn't join them. Put it on your late-night drinking list – opening hours here run from dusk to way past your bedtime. Cobblestones, lanterns and small illuminated signs will draw you into the street's timeless magic. Many eateries here open out onto yuka (dining platforms), and in the summer months you can laze by the riverside, with views of beautiful Gion and the Kamo River's many impressive bridges.

Be brave; you may be turned away from many of the exclusive establishments in this neighbourhood, but adventure is lurking down alleys and up or down stairways – and after a drink or two you might find yourself channeling your inner samurai or wannabe geisha. Seedy bars, eye-bogglingly expensive bills, the gaudy, the crass and the simply beautiful – you'll find it all here in an authentic (and at times questionably authentic) slice of old Kyoto.

KYOTO IMPERIAL PALACE

Further north from Teramachi, things start to get very peaceful – as the vast parklands of Kyoto Imperial Palace take over, a great spot for picnicking or cycling, or to view cherry blossoms when in season. The surrounding Kyoto Gyoen garden is a sprawling park, and a popular spot to view both cherry blossoms and the colours of autumn.

In recent times the area around the Imperial Palace gardens has experienced a revival – and coffee houses, antique shops, young designer boutiques and small maker stores can be found here. You'll also find the Raku Museum (see p. 202) that explores the raku philosophy of pottery.

NOTABLE NEIGHBOURHOODS

NIJO CASTLE

Presided over by ancient and proud Nijo Castle (see p. 203), one of Kyoto's most popular attractions, Nijo is an area of stark contrasts. Open boulevards and residential blocks are punctuated by laneways that hide cool new additions to Kyoto's retail and eating experiences. This is a place for walking and discovering. Wherever you go, the expansive castle grounds will be in sight – the high walls offering tantalising glimpses of what lies beyond. You can only enter the castle grounds from the east. As you do, you can admire the wide moat that defends the castle from attack, although the only assault these days comes from busloads of tourists.

You're in ninja territory now, so slip into side streets and sneak into buildings to uncover contemporary Nijo. Sidle into antique stores to unearth some gems from Kyoto's distant past. Pad quietly into old townhouses that have been turned into exciting new eateries, or blend silently into your surroundings in contemporary coffee shops and stores that put a new spin on traditional Kyoto.

GION

In Gion you'll be transported into Kyoto's rich and golden past, where geisha and maiko (apprentice geisha) rushed from one appointment to the next, well-to-do families shopped for the most exquisite products, and small stores with generations of owners still ply their trade today. As you cross Shijo Bridge and the grand Minamiza Kabuki Theatre (see p. 205) comes into view, you'll find yourself wafting into the heart of Gion, gateway to Higashiyama and many of Kyoto's most popular temples and shrines, like Kennin-ji temple (see p. 187). You're in Kyoto's heartland here: a world populated by picture postcard-preserved machiya (traditional wooden townhouses), cobbled streets, noren (traditional fabric curtains) and beautiful lanterns. On Hanamikoji-dori, you can still see geisha getting into a taxi or hopping onto a rickshaw on their way to a performance or making an important delivery with a perfectly wrapped bundle in hand. Ochaya (tea houses) still perform the traditional tea ceremony, and notable restaurants in machiya excel in kaiseki ryori (refined, multi-course cuisine).

With delicate, refined food, longstanding dessert houses, traditional shops and a vast range of souvenirs, Gion is the Kyoto you've dreamt of.

NISHIJIN

Bordered by the Nijo Castle area, Kita Oji station and Kyoto's atmospheric north, Nishijin is a haven from the city centre, an up-and-coming area where tradition and modernity blend into a cohesive amalgam of old-world craftmanship and new technology. Nishijin is best known for its textiles, a particular textile to be precise: the Nishijin-oji, a richly decorated woven fabric with silk thread that's highly regarded throughout the country. After the Onin war in 1477, many weavers who had fled to various corners of Japan returned to Kyoto. Their main hub was Nishijin, and it is estimated that there are now over 465 fabric vendors there. The history can be experienced first-hand and can be seen in the streets around Imadegawa-Ōmiya and Imadegawa-Horikawa and in the displays at the Nishijin Textile Center (see p. 206).

A younger demographic has repurposed old houses and buildings here, creating a clutch of contemporary cafes and stores. Many of the stores sell modern versions of traditional crafts, refurbished antiques and vintage goods, or use traditional techniques for making sweets. All of this makes Nishijin the perfect neighbourhood to uncover Kyoto's patchwork, textile heart.

SOUTH HIGASHIYAMA

The southern part of the Higashiyama mountain ranges in the eastern corner of Kyoto is one of the prime destinations for Kyoto daytrippers, a snap-happy wonderland of 'oohh' and 'aahh' moments showcasing many places of astounding beauty and enormous cultural significance. It will be day one for

NOTABLE NEIGHBOURHOODS

many visitors to Kyoto, who will wend their way through Gion to Yasaka shrine and onto the pilgrimage-like, preserved streets of Ninen-zaka and Sanen-zaka. An abundance of beautiful shrines, gardens, walkways and longstanding eateries and stores will lead you to your ultimate destination – the stunning temple of Kyomizu-dera (see p. 157), standing proudly on its high, thick wooden stilts. Unmissable sights include the Hokan-ji pagoda (see p. 71), the oft-missed Kodai-ji (see p. 190) and sub-temple Entoku-in, beautiful Ishibel-koji lane and Sanjusangendo that features over 1000 Kannon (Buddhist goddess of mercy) statues.

South Higashiyama holds the key to Kyoto's combined power of iconic monuments and ancient Zen-like calm.

NORTH HIGASHIYAMA

As you head out of Gion and into Higashiyama, the mountain air fills your lungs, the scenery starts to change, and the atmosphere is tranquil and leisurely. Stunning temple and shrine experiences are plentiful, and with more destinations off the tourist bus route, chances are you'll find yourself alone in some of the most beautiful places on earth. From peaceful Zen Buddhist temple Nanzen-ji (see p. 172), you can walk in quiet contemplation, as locals and monks have for many years, along the Philosopher's Path (see p. 18), a prime-viewing spot for cherry blossoms during hanami (cherry blossom season). The path takes you to the popular Ginkaku-ji (Silver temple, see p. 21) and its perfectly manicured gardens. North Higashiyama is also where you'll find the towering vermillion torii gate that leads to the Heian-jingu shrine (see p. 158), whose garden is home to the stepping-stones made famous by a contemplative Scarlett Johansson in *Lost in Translation*. Wander through the maze-like temple complex of Chion-in (see p. 193) and head up the impossibly steep stairs to find the melancholy temple of bells.

Over the past five years a vibrant shopping and cafe scene and stores exhibiting an eclectic mix of old- and new-school wares has given the traditional back streets a contemporary edge, adding to the area's allure.

DEMACHIYANAGI

Demachiyanagi is a breezy university town where some of Kyoto's coolest shops and restaurants can be found butting up against longstanding eateries and cafes, and students tuck into vegetarian meals and drink excellent coffee while swapping ideas and sharing philosophies. Demachiyanagi sits on the Kamogawa Delta, the point where the Kamo River gets into its own heated philosophical debate, splits into two schools of thought and heads into the mountains. It's a great neighbourhood in which to grab coffee or breakfast, or to hit a burger or falafel joint or a bar at night, and the perfect base camp for a daytrip on the Eizan line which runs north towards Kurama, Kibune and Mount Hiei (see p. 219).

If you're exploring the shrines and temples of Kyoto, you won't want to miss Shimogamo. A sanctuary within a deep green forest on the Kamagawa Delta, this is the oldest Shinto shrine in Kyoto, dating back to the 6th century CE.

ARASHIYAMA

Arashiyama has it all – and this might explain its staggering popularity. The famous Togetsu 'Moon Crossing' Bridge has great mountain views with autumnal foliage, cherry blossoms or blankets of snow, depending on the season. You'll frequently find yourself swatting your way through gnat-like clouds of wonder-struck excursionists, but they are there for a reason. The Sagano Bamboo Grove (see p. 160) is an unmissable experience, and strolling through this impressive forest of towering bamboo trees is an Arashiyama rite of passage. There are endless photo opportunities in the grove, but pictures won't do justice to the deep smell of wood and dirt, and the wonderful stillness.

The neighbourhood also boasts one of Kyoto's most expansive, and to our minds, most impressive, temple grounds. Tenryu-ji (see p. 163) is a Rinzai Buddhist complex complete with a memorable garden and a popular restaurant specialising in shojin-ryori (vegetarian banquet). At Arashiyama Station, you'll find the popular Kimono Forest (see p. 29).

Arashiyama feels like a daytrip, but it's not far from Kyoto at all – so make sure you don't miss everything this extraordinary neighbourhood has to offer.

NORTH KYOTO

North Kyoto is having a moment. The Golden Pavilion at Kinkaku-ji temple (see p. 178), brings people flocking to this area, but they rarely stay to explore. For those in the know, however, this is the poster neighbourhood for the reinvention of Kyoto, taking ancient traditional beauty and spinning it for the current day. It's a brave new world – Omiya-dori is dotted with unique cafes built into beautiful ancient buildings, shops sell contemporary handcrafted items, and eateries give classic Kyoto cuisine a new twist. Students are driving the influx of vegetarian cafes, sweet shops and burger joints. The old world still stakes a claim, with markets on the grounds of spectacular temples, antique and vintage stores crammed with oddments and relics, one-of-a-kind Kyoto craft experiences and some longstanding eateries that have perfected many aspects of Kyoto cuisine over time.

The encroachment of the contemporary world is imminent here, although its seamless blending with Kyoto's ancient splendour is remarkable. Temple fanatics note: north Kyoto also has an unmissable complex, sprawling Daitoku-ji temple.

PHILOSOPHER'S PATH
FULL-DAY ITINERARY

People travel to Kyoto to search for an inner peace or to absorb calm through daily walks, temple prayers and meditation. The Philosopher's Path is a beautiful canal-side stroll which connects two areas of great historical significance. A day walking along the path, exploring the temples and gardens at each end, will take you to some of Kyoto's true treasures; make sure you tap into sources of that deep, spiritual energy.

8 AM Catch the Tozai line to ① **Keage station**. Leave from exit 2. If you are visiting in cherry blossom season, walk the ② **Keage Incline**, beating the crowds to immerse yourself in a sea of pink.

9.30 AM The ③ **Nanzen-ji temple complex** (see p. 172) is really a half-day's itinerary on its own, with several stunning gardens, an aqueduct, tearoom and the unmissable, ancient Sanmon gate. We love to wander Nanzen-ji's main grounds, a tranquil stroll around stunning wooden buildings and moss carpeted gardens, breathing air heavy with incense and the seasonal perfume of the many plants and flowers. Sub-temple Tenjuan has a memorable garden complete with a pond, traversed by steppingstones. The northern Hojo has a dry garden dating back to the Edo period (1603 to 1867). If you are lucky enough to hear the bells tolling, you'll know the monks are at prayer. (The bells also ring at dusk, which is a spectacular time to visit Nanzen-ji.)

11 AM Just a short stroll to Nanzen-ji's west is one of Kyoto's prettiest Buddhist temples, ④ **Eikan-do (Zenrin-ji) temple** (see p. 171). Explore the colourful temple, steep canopied spiral staircase, towering mountainside pagoda and beautiful, expansive water garden.

12.30 PM Now you are in a mindful mood, start to make your ascent to the Philosopher's Path. Pop into to ⑤ **Flower Green Days** (see p. 43) for a middle of the day fortifying coffee (lunch comes a little later) amongst a sea of dried flowers. From here, keep walking up the hill until you reach the beginning of the Philosopher's Path. Wander the narrow path next to the canal that has weeping trees bending over the gently burbling waters as if in prayer. Veer off left and right when something takes your fancy (we always visit Bild, a wonderful antique store off the beaten path) and peer down roads and over bridges to discover hidden enclaves and temples. One of our favourite stores, ⑥ **Kiso Artech** (see p. 128) is always a must-visit for perfectly carved wooden household items.

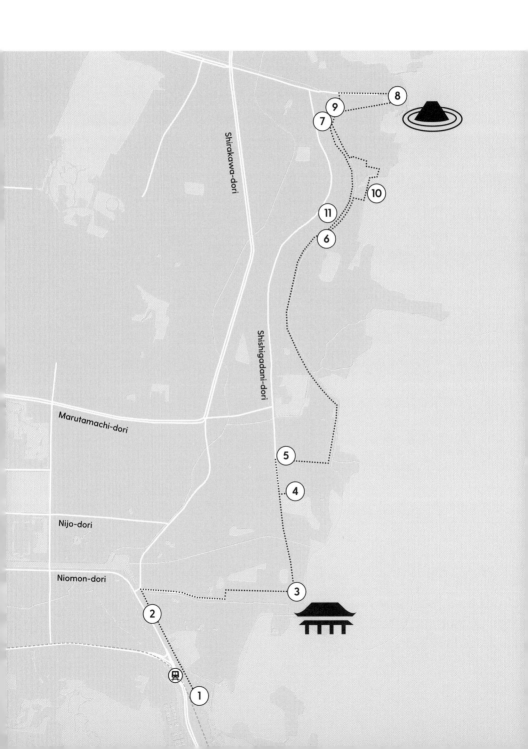

2PM Have a late lunch of perfect, chewy, handmade noodles at ⑦ **Omen** (see p. 74), where you'll eat some of the city's best udon.

3PM After lunch, at the opposite end of the Philosopher's Path to Nanzen-ji temple you'll find another splendid temple, ⑧ **Jisho-ji temple**, best known as GInkaku-ji temple, or the Silver temple. Take time to explore the beautiful garden, walking high onto the hill to get a spectacular view of Kyoto. The sand mound here is said to represent Mount Fuji, especially when reflected in the waters of the pond. The temple itself is from the 15th century, beautiful, but sadly not clad in silver due to a lack of funds.

4.30PM Start walking back along the Philosopher's Path as the sunlight begins to fade. Refuel with coffee at ⑨ **Brown Eyes Coffee** before visiting ⑩ **Honen-in temple**, a secret temple often ignored by tourists. Walk through the tranquil garden within before once more returning to the path.

6PM Time for an early dinner at ⑪ **Monk**, a moody pizzeria with one of the world's best locations, a quiet spot on the Philosopher's Path itself. Gaze out onto the path as dusk descends, enjoying wood-fired pizza and seasonal delights (book in advance).

8PM Cap off your day with an atmospheric walk back to Keage station, meditating upon your newly forged philosophies and newfound inner tranquillity.

STEVE'S VINYL HUNTING, BRUTALISM, BOOKS & BARS

FULL-DAY ITINERARY

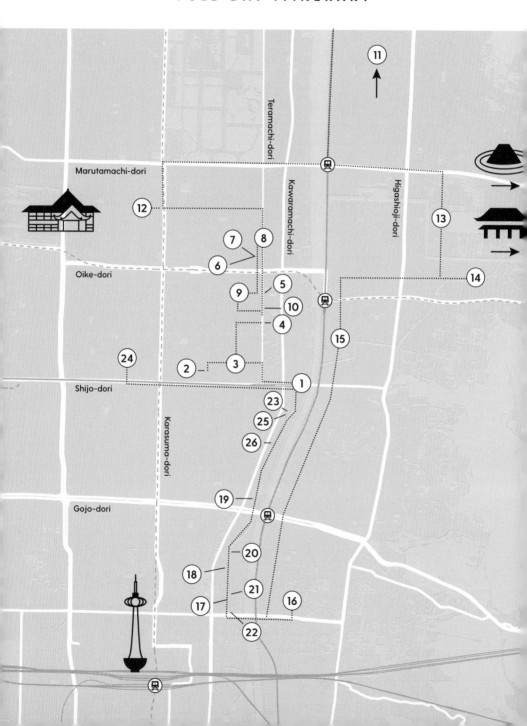

If a day of vinyl hunting, Brutalism (a functional form of architecture unusual to Kyoto), books and bars appeals, then this itinerary is most definitely for you. I've clustered the listings so all the vinyl hunting, architecture, volumes, food and tipples are grouped together, however freestyle your way around my itinerary if you so desire. As the daylight fades, taking your time along the canals, flanked by small cafes and bars run by locals and brimming with character.

9AM I like to start the day in style, perhaps with an old-school kissaten (retro coffee house) coffee and breakfast set at chic ① **Salon de thé François** (see p. 37).

10AM It's time for some vintage vinyl record shopping while taking in some traditional Kyoto buys as well. I head to ② **Joe's Garage** first, just off Shijo-dori, and assault the record racks for some classic experimental rock. Then I stroll through ③ **Nishiki Market** (see p. 63), marvelling at the colours and shapes of sweets, pickles and assorted seafood skewers. Afterwards, I head north, popping in to ④ **Poco a Poco** (see p. 117) and then ⑤ **Happy Jack** (see p. 117) for more crate digging. Further north over busy Oike-dori in the more tranquil, uncovered part of Teramachi-dori, I'll search out more vintage vinyl finds in the Morris Building at ⑥ **100000t alonetoco**, and one floor above, ⑦ **Workshop Records** (see p. 117). Not much further up you'll find ⑧ **Hard Bop** records (see p. 117), a must for jazz and bluenote fiends.

1PM Head back down Teramachi-dori to Sanjo-dori, where it's time to pop into ⑨ **Cafe Indépendants** (see p. 59) for a breezy 'Western style' lunch and a cheeky beer in a quirky building that dates to 1928. Follow up with a taiyaki, a filled pastry treat shaped like a fish, at ⑩ **Naruto Taiyaki Honpo**.

2.30PM Brutalism is having a moment in Kyoto and if you're a fan of the mid-20th-century's imposing grey bunkers, you'll want to head north to marvel at the stark angles and monolithic scope of Sachio Otani's ⑪ **Kyoto International Conference Centre**. For more fun with concrete buildings, head south-west for Kazumasa Yamashita's playful ⑫ **Face House**. To the east of here you'll find ⑬ the **Rohm Theatre** (see p. 208), an unforgiving fortress in concrete and glass, once nearly demolished, now restored and housing popular bookstore Tsutaya. If, like me, you like the musty smell of yellowed paper and the feel of old pages between your fingers, explore the small vintage bookstores of the area, including ⑭ **Art Books Yamazaki** and ⑮ **Books & Things**.

Itinerary

3.30PM I have a sweet tooth and I'm sure many readers can sympathise. About now the blood sugar is running low, so let's make our way down further south to longstanding charmer (16) **Shichijo Kanshundo** (see p. 95). Tuck into a voluminous matcha parfait while admiring the small garden through sliding shoji windows.

4.30PM Time for one of my favourite Kyoto experiences: a tranquil stroll along the (17) **Takase River Canal**. I usually head north. The stroll takes in many traditional and historical buildings and gives you a glimpse of local Kyoto going quietly about its business. Gather afternoon fuel at (18) **Murmur Coffee** and pop into adorable (19) **2eme MAISON** for some cherry pie and a cocktail. Admire the cute frontage of retro (20) **Ume-yu bathhouse** (enjoy a soak if you're feeling weary). Continue north and pop in and out of the tiny bars and mingle with the locals. My picks are (21) **Kyoto Beer Lab**, (22) **Craft House Kyoto** and/or (23) **Turquoise Bar** – they'll all be open by now.

7PM From here I meet Michelle and we roll into (24) **AWOMB Kurasuma Honten** (see p. 56) for hand-rolled sushi (pre-booking recommended). Then we finish the day with elaborate drinks at (25) **L'Escamoteur** or (26) **Bar Reloom**. Exhausted, laden with records, with a full belly and a dizzy head, we'll head back to the hotel, having had the best day ever.

MICHELLE'S CRAFT & DESIGN

FULL-DAY ITINERARY

Spending a day wandering my favourite local Kyoto haunts is a slow reveal of the city's rich history, a pageant of emperors, samurai and craftspeople. I love to visit museums and shops run by local makers, or dig through ramshackle antique markets and vintage stores. Elegant and detailed art and craft skills go hand in hand with the beauty of the city's temples and gardens. A day exploring the aesthetic history of Kyoto will certainly inspire you in your own creative endeavours.

7 AM I always start the day with a hot bath! My prerequisite in booking a hotel is that it has to have a public bath so I can start my morning in a contemplative way. I buy a dorayaki (small pancake filled with sweet bean paste) from a konbini (convenience store) or a Departo food hall to have in my room with a cup of tea. I will often take my visual journal so I can write about or sketch my surroundings throughout the day.

8 AM Atmospheric UNESCO World Heritage Site ① **To-ji temple** (see p. 154) opens at 8am and an early morning walk around the grounds and majestic buildings is a calming start to the day. It's home to an unmissable Kobo-ichi flea market (on the 21st of each month) and a 'junk market' called Garakuta-ichi (the first Sun of every month). The closest station to To-ji temple is Toji station, however I will often walk there from Kyoto station (it's a 15min walk).

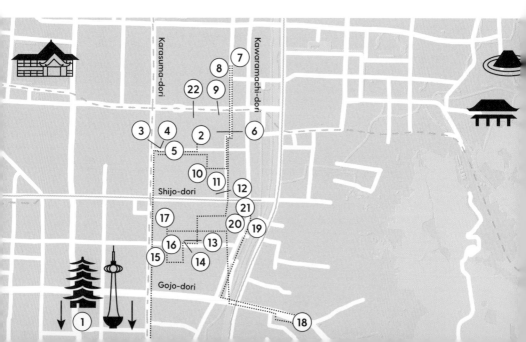

10AM Walk from To-ji temple to Kujo station or Kyoto station (both around 15min) and catch the train to Karasuma Oike station, exit 5 for the Viennese coffee and a tamago (egg) sandwich at ② **Inoda Coffee Honten** (see p. 155).

11.30AM–1PM I spend a couple of hours wandering the nearby streets, especially historic Rokaku-dori. I float into ③ **Rokkaku-do temple (Choho-ji)** (see p. 163) and visit the Ikebana store ④ **Karaku** (see p. 112) on the 8th floor of the Ikenobo Headquarters Building. I stop for wagashi (Japanese sweets) at ⑤ **Seien Daigokudenhompo** (see p. 139) and visit ⑥ **Miyawaki Baisen-an** fan store. Then I walk up Teramachi-dori to buy tea at ⑦ **Ippodo** (see p. 142), browse at ⑧ **Zohiko Urushi Art** (see p. 118) for lacquerware, and admire the stationery at ⑨ **Kyukyodo** (see p. 143). I make my way back down Teramachi-dori towards Shijo-dori, veering off to visit ⑩ **SOWGEN** (see p. 113), uncovering paraphernalia liberated from Kyoto's past. Then it's back onto Teramachi-dori to visit old-school ⑪ **Horaido** (see p. 117) for the heady scent of genmaicha (roasted rice tea – they invented it here!) and, if I need some sugar, I head to Shinkyogoku for donuts at ⑫ **Koé Donuts Kyoto**.

1PM By now I'm hungry, so I head to ⑬ **D&Department** (see p. 107), on the grounds of Bukko-ji temple, who offer lunch sets in a beautiful room.

2PM After lunch, I pop over to ⑭ **D&Department Design Store** on the same grounds to peruse the selection of clothing and homewares. It's a short walk from here to ⑮ **kitone** (see p. 108), a tiny store that houses a beautiful collection of handmade items. My next destination is ⑯ **Saryo Suisen** (see p. 87), for a matcha and a parfait, before I head towards old-school paper merchant ⑰ **Morita Washi** to admire their elaborate sheets of artisan paper.

3.30PM From here it's a short walk (or catch a cab) to meander your way through the backstreets of South Higashiyama to the mid-century master potter's house turned museum ⑱ **Kawai Kanjiro's House** (see p. 207). This hidden treasure is a must-see (it shuts at 5pm, with last entry at 4.30pm).

5PM After this I walk 20min along the Kamo River, crossing at the Donguri Dori bridge to visit the sublime ⑲ **minä perhonen** (see p. 109) store housed in an exquisite mid-century building. Not far from here I'll duck into ⑳ **Rau** (see p. 88) for a late-afternoon treat: a unique blended tea and an incredible sweet sculpture. (If you are tired after such a busy day, pick up one of the beautiful healthy bentos from ㉑ **Good Nature Station** for a hotel room picnic, see p. 88).

7PM As the lights dim on another day in Kyoto, I head to ㉒ **Chisou Inaseya** (see p. 53), a beautiful machiya (townhouse) for delicious food and sake.

MINDFUL DAY
FULL-DAY ITINERARY

A long history of spirituality and mindful practice has made Kyoto one of the world's best destinations for anyone wanting to reset their inner self. From morning prayers and meditation in longstanding temples to artisan craft classes and soaking in the hot, healing waters of an onsen, Kyoto will make sure that you are centred, balanced and revitalised.

You can stay overnight at a one- or three-day Zen and wellbeing retreat at the guesthouse at ① **Shunko-in in Myoshin-ji temple** (see p. 163).

SUNRISE Take in early morning prayers and have a vegetarian breakfast at Shunko-in. Tip: it is a good idea to send bags to your next hotel with Yamato courier so you are unencumbered for the day and don't have to return to the temple to get your bags.

10AM Explore the expansive temple grounds at Shunko-in in Myoshin-ji, and head into a sub temple within the grounds, ② **Taizo-in** to see the white and black dry gardens. Make sure you visit their teahouse for matcha and wagashi (Japanese sweets) and participate in Taizo-in's calligraphy class. (The main Myoshin-ji complex also offers zazen meditation and a tea ceremony).

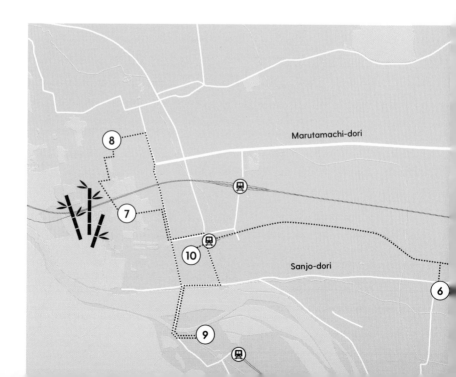

12PM Stop at ③ **Ajiro** (see p. 185) for a vegan shojin ryori set lunch bento. Ajiro is just outside the temple grounds and bookings are a must.

1.30PM Walk to Myōshinji station and catch the train one stop to Ryoanji station.

2PM Walk to ④ **Ryoan-ji temple** (see p. 163), stopping for a tea ceremony at ⑤ **Camellia Tea Ceremony Garden** (see p. 163). Explore Ryoan-ji's beautiful temple and gardens, stopping to take particular note of the famous Zen rock garden.

3PM Head back to Ryoanji station and catch the train to Arisugawa station, then walk to ⑥ **Sagano Onsen Tenzan No Yu** and soak the afternoon away. Alternatively, catch the train to Arashiyama station and head to ⑦ **Tenryu-ji temple** (see p. 173) to explore the vast gardens and sign up for a sutra copying class. Exit to the north of the temple grounds to take a leisurely stroll through the bamboo grove. Visit nearby ⑧ **Rakushisha** (see p. 196), once home to Basho disciple Mukai Kyorai, and compose your own Haiku.

6PM Head to ⑨ **Pizzeria Mama** (see p. 75) for dinner (this is also a hotel and booking online is a must). Head back to Arashiyama station to walk through the ⑩ **Kimono Forest**, with its 600 poles covered with 32 differently patterned fabrics, which look wonderful when lit up at night.

珈琲と喫茶店

COFFEE & KISSATEN

A blend of cosy old-world kissaten (vintage coffee houses) and contemporary cafes set up in machiya (traditional wooden townhouses) have made Kyoto one of the world's most eclectic and vibrant coffee destinations.

Kissaten started popping up in the early Showa period (1926–89) when coffee was introduced to Japan. These owner/ operator relics are retro-cool time capsules with a collision of stylistic elements from mid-century to post-war Americana, Parisien Belle Epoch and Swiss chalet chic. Expect shelves of bottled coffee beans and vintage crockery, retro lighting, grandfather clocks, booth-style seating and tables draped in '60s British cafe lace, all soundtracked by smooth jazz or classical music. The 'Kissa' coffee menu includes Americano and Viennese coffee and café au lait. Drip coffee is the staple for morning sets (breakfast) and cake sets.

Kyoto's new wave of coffee houses occupy spaces like works of art (see Walden Woods Kyoto, p. 33 or Blend Kyoto, p. 40). Others are set up in sleek architecturally-designed buildings in notable tourists areas. Aim for a cafe that suits your style or piques your interest. Some are in the city centre, like Salon de thè François (see p. 37) or master-piece coffee (see p. 35) and some are further out, like the classic Coffee House Maki (see p. 219) or the striking Bread, Espresso & Arashiyama Garden (see p. 44).

Walden Woods Kyoto
ウォールデン ウッズ キョウト

A contemporary Zen space for contemplating coffee.

Found in the backstreets of Kyoto not far from Kyoto station, Walden Woods is a neo-modernist, surrealist white cube that manages to be out of time and place while perfectly encapsulating the minimalist spirit and delicate beauty of the city. Its stark interior beckons you into a world where you are invited to sip coffee in an imagined forest in the snow. The titular 'woods' is a stark theatre-in-the-round, an ampitheatre where your fellow coffee addicts are the audience watching a caffeinated drama in which you are the hapless dependent. The vivid space is a blank canvas that evokes the solitude of Thoreau's novel *Walden*.

It's unlikely that Thoreau could get a decent coffee alone in the woods, but here you are in luck. Choose from the classics, including Americano, espresso or latte (plant-based drinkers can order theirs with soy milk). Matcha latte and chai are also on the menu, however it's the pour-over Walden Woods original single-origin and blend coffees (their beans are roasted on site) their disciples flock here for. We ordered their original blend pour-over, ginger syrup latte which came in their signature cups delivered on a tin tray, along with their fruit sandwich. Make sure to buy some Walden Wolf Blend beans and a candle, so you can attempt to re-create the experience at home.

508-1 Sakaecho
Shimogyo-ku

344 9009

Gojo

Mon–Sun 9am–6pm

JP¥
¥

W
walden-woods.com

Good Time Coffee
グッドタイムコーヒー

A petite wooden cube dispensing coffee, with its own craft market.

357 Tsukinuke
Shimogyo-ku

202 7824

Umekoji-Kyotonishi

Mon–Sun 10am–5pm

JP¥
¥

W
goodtime.coffee

If you're exploring the south part of Kyoto between Kyoto station and Gojo, you'll come across a puzzle-box coffee stand serving takeaway drip coffee through various sliding wooden windows. Staff magically appear and disappear to select from premium roasted beans before materialising again in front of you with a perfectly forged brew. Opt for a perky latte with ginger or caramel syrup to takeaway, or head inside to the minimal room where artfully placed, repurposed school furniture overlooks a small garden. Tea, soft drinks, Kyoto beer and fruit sandwiches are also on the menu. We opted for a robust Ethiopian blend drip coffee and a caramel latte to accompany a kamonegi sandwich stuffed full of duck, shimeji and scallions. Owner Murata set the cafe up in a townhouse that's over 100 years old and many of the original features are preserved. They also run a craft market of sorts upstairs, selling up-cycled traditional fabrics, clothing, giftware, homewares, plants and pre-loved kimono. Don't forget to visit Good Time Coffee's Higashiyama store.

master-piece coffee
マスターピース コーヒー

A secret, cosy cafe and enchanting garden on one of Kyoto's most charming shopping strips.

26 Nakanocho
Nakagyo-ku

231 6828

Kyoto Shiyakusho-mae

Mon–Sun 11am–6pm

JP¥

¥

W

master-piece.co.jp

You could easily stroll past this excellent coffee spot, so look for the striking Meiji period (1868–1912) frontage of Marcourt on Sanjo-dori and enter the alley directly across the street. At the back of master-piece leather and waterproof goods store, you'll find a small right-angle sliver of a cafe that makes exceptional coffee and sandwiches. Slip off your shoes and slide into a window seat that boasts a view of a stunning traditional garden, especially atmospheric in autumn when the central maple is a vibrant red. Count the various varieties of moss while the bamboo pipe on the chozubachi (water bowl) drips meditatively. We ordered the matcha latte and a seasonal chestnut latte. The tamago (egg) sandwich, a delicious update of the kissaten staple, features two perfectly soft-boiled eggs cut in half and placed in the sliced sandwich 'sunny side out' for full effect. Desserts include a chocolate marble cheesecake and an affogato, or have a Heartland or Moretti beer as you watch the daylight dim and the lights come on, illuminating the beautiful garden.

Coffee & kissaten

Salon de thé François

フランソア喫茶室

A touch of French elegance with a Japanese twist in a longstanding cafe.

Salon de thé François is a French cafe in a parallel universe. Since its inception in 1934, it has garnered a well-earned reputation as one of the most sophisticated tea and coffee houses in Japan. Named after artist François Millet, the association seems to stop there. The exterior has an almost church-like feel with gothic arched doors and stained-glass windows. Inside, chandeliers, vaulted ceilings and church pews add to the spiritual atmosphere, while red velvet couches lend an air of glamour. Relax in the main room under the lavish domed ceiling or hide around the corner where girlfriends catch up in cosy booths, couples share desserts on sweetheart bench seats or long-time patrons slowly stir their café au lait, Americano with cream or Vienna coffee. Delicate triangle sandwiches, tartlettes and brûlées are on the menu. Charming coffee cups feature the cafe's logo and a French flag – in case you hadn't worked out the theme.

If you're there in the morning, the toast sets (ham, egg, pizza topping or cinnamon sugar) are the perfect breakfast. In the afternoons, indulge in a coffee float or cuddle up with a brandy. You won't quite feel like you're in Paris's Latin Quarter, but this Kyoto blend of chic, breezy and lost-in-time ambience has its own charm. The prices match its place in history and as a registered Cultural Tangible Property we think it's worth every yen.

184 Sendocho
Shimogyo-ku

351 4042

Kyoto-Kawaramachi

Mon–Sun 10am–10pm

JPY
¥¥

W
francois1934.com

Coffee & kissaten

Soirée
喫茶ソワレ

Over-the-top retro chic in an unmissable kissaten.

95-5 Shin-Cho Nishi-
kiyamachi-dori
Shijo-agaru Shimogyo-ku

221 0351

Kyoto-Kawaramachi

Tues–Sun 12pm–10pm

JP¥

¥¥

W

soiree-kyoto.com

Emperor Showa reigned from the 1920s until the '80s, and this post–World War II cafe and ex-sweets shop has a bit of every decade of the Showa period thrown in. Two cosy floors showcase a clutter of mock medieval ornate wood panelling, statuettes, hanging mirrors, chandeliers and faux '70s light fixtures that cast a lurid glow over the green vinyl benches. The clientele runs the whole gamut of locals, from friends out for the afternoon to businessmen taking a break to lunching ladies. Pop-culture fanatics and the curious tourist will find it a mesmerising experience. It's gloriously chintzy, and although the menu is not in English, there are plenty of pictures of luminescent jelly drinks or over-the-top cakes and parfaits to point to. If you're a Kyoto-ite, chances are your grandparents came here on a date, and now it's your turn.

Rokuyosha
六曜社

A time capsule coffee house hiding in plain sight on a main street.

40-1 Daikokucho
Nakagyo-ku

241 3026

Sanjo

Mon–Tues & Thurs–Sun
8.30am–10pm

JP¥

¥

W

rokuyosha-cofee.com

This longstanding kissaten (vintage coffee house) has been on busy Kawaramachi-dori since the 1950s. The vintage browns and faded tiles of the entrance are telling – it has weathered the encroachment of modernity (and style) to emerge as both a curiosity and a recommended stop for coffee. The brews here are classic kissaten fare; we chose a café au lait and the iced house-blended coffee, paired with one of their renowned donuts and a dainty Swiss roll. Their morning sets of brewed coffee served in the finest vintage porcelain with big toast and eggs is the perfect post-BNO (big night out) remedy. Relax on beige vinyl banquettes admiring '70s glazed orange tiles, wood parquetry walls, Wedgewood crockery, wall clocks and African statuettes. Lights glow dimly making it a cosy cocoon, shutting out the noise and glare of the outside world. The downstairs room (the original coffee shop) opens in the afternoon and morphs into a bar where locals gather for some post-war Kyoto vibes. Don't forget to souvenir one of their iconic matchboxes.

Coffee & kissaten

Blend Kyoto
ブレンドキョウト

Typography and coffee are a match made in heaven.

---

447 Sasayacho
Nakagyo-ku

285 4268

Marutamachi

Mon–Fri 11am–6pm, Sat–Sun
10am–6pm

JP¥

¥¥

W

blend.kyoto

A dark minimalist wooden box waits for you on a tranquil street, perfectly situated near the Imperial Palace Gardens and northern Teramachi-dori. This one-man-show cafe is classic slow Kyoto, where the time taken and the process of the coffee being made is an essential part of the experience. If you want to grab a quick and impersonal coffee on the go, then this isn't the place for you. A very serious and effortlessly cool clientele choose from a range of coffee named after classic typefaces: Helvetica, Baskerville and Optima. Step one, take in the aroma of each canister to find your preference (you can even blend favourites for your own signature coffee). Step two, order and then relax while your spiritual barista goes about slowly creating your rich black coffee, which comes in a scientific beaker, a slow pour-over creation made for you to savour. Step three, make sure to take note of the message at the bottom of your glass when you finish. There is limited seating, so be patient and maybe you'll be able to seat yourself at the low bench by the darkly painted and impressively sourced tree trunk.

Usagi Coffee
兎珈琲

Cafes are breeding like rattbits in Kyoto.

27-1 Oshiboricho
Nakagyo-ku

708 8899

Nijojo-mae

Mon–Sun 10am–7pm

JP¥
¥

W
instagram.com/_usagicoffee

A short stroll from the majesty of Nijo Castle (see p. 205), Usagi Coffee is a contemporary concrete bunker in a 1920's machiya (traditional wooden townhouse), warmed up by rope noren (traditional fabric curtains) adorning the exterior, a suspended rabbit mask and a dark wood staircase and large rear windows which look out onto a tsuboniwa (small Japanese garden). Staff wear graphic print uniforms with rabbit masks and can make you the perfect latte or a batch of must-buy rabbit-shaped castella cake bites, served in small bags emblazoned with the cute rabbit logo (you will have worked out by now that 'usagi' means rabbit). The walls are lined with Usagi Coffee's products: coffee beans, shopping bags, fans, ceramics and hoodies. We ordered a matcha latte, organic apple juice and, of course, some cute and delicious castella. They also serve a charcoal latte, if you're keen to try the latest fad. If the merchandise appeals, visit the specialty shop at the end of the tsuboniwa's stepping stones.

Clamp Coffee Sarasa
クランプコーヒー サラサ

Coffee and chats are a serious business here.

67-38 Nishinokyo Shokushicho
Nakagyo-ku

822 9397

Nijojo-mae

Mon–Sun 11am–6pm

JP¥
¥

W
cafe-sarasa.com

The enclave around Clamp Coffee is a charming, leafy cul-de-sac with several browse-worthy stores. Clamp Coffee is perched in the middle and caters to a dedicated local clientele. Walls and shelves are cluttered with mismatched Americana (the US flag greets you as you enter), but don't expect a caramel latte or frappuccino. Coffee here is pour-over, single origin, and they take their time getting it right. The cafe only seats about 12, with most of the space in the room taken up by a huge (functioning) coffee bean roaster. They sell bags of their expertly roasted beans, so you can take a bit of Clamp home with you. Join the communal table or take a chair by the window and sip excellent coffee to a soundtrack of American country and blues. The wall says it all: 'One of the great joys in life is coffee and good conversation.'

Flower Green Days
フラワーグリーンデイズ

Pause between temples for Italian coffee amongst floral beauty.

2-2-4 Nyakuojicho
Sakyo-ku

Keage

Mon–Sun 12.30pm-5pm

JP¥

¥

W
flowergreendays.stores.jp

If you are looking for coffee amongst the flowers between Eikan-dō (see p. 171) and the eastern entrance to the Philosopher's Path (see p. 19), Flower Green Days is perfectly placed. The 'shou sugi ban' burnt wood box accentuates the winding green vine tendrils and a classic Kyoto potted garden. A chic cafe and flower shop, the interior embodies strength meets fragility, where concrete and wood showcase gently dried blooms that are suspended from the ceiling, forming a vividly coloured cave. Owner Misa Osawa makes some of the most beautiful wreaths and arrangements with dried flowers, seed pods and cones, and small potpourri bottles, which make an elegant and tasteful gift if you have a host or friend in Kyoto that you would like to treat. Perch yourself on one of their window benches and sip a latte or tea soda. Osawa-san's baked treat of choice is the perfect accompaniment. We tried the peanut butter cookie with an espresso, while sitting on the outside bench getting philosophical before our stroll on the Philosopher's Path.

Coffee & kissaten

Bread, Espresso & Arashiyama Garden
パンとエスプレッソと嵐山庭園

A bakery and an enchanting dessert house in a peaceful Arashiyama backstreet.

45-15 Sagatenryuji
Susukinobabachu
Ukyo-ku

432 7940

Arashiyama

Mon–Sun 10am–6pm

JP¥
¥¥

W
bread-espresso.jp

Only a 5min walk from busy Randen Arashiyama station, you'll find a calm street where two buildings sit astride a beautiful island garden. The Bread, Espresso part of the equation is a small bakery set in a dark wooden building where staff in chic uniforms emblazoned with their illustrative logo dispense fruit bread and shokopan (Japanese milk bread), which you watch being kneaded and baked through a window. Strictly a takeaway venue, join the queue and choose from an array of baked delights (we chose the matcha cream bun and matcha melon pan). Opposite, Arashiyama Garden is a popular spot for couples, and is housed in the former Kobayashi Villa, a dark wooden, farmhouse-style building with an impressive, thickly thatched roof. Sign into the digital guest list outside and be prepared to wait. Once inside we sat on zabuton (cushions) overlooking the beautiful garden, and ordered the matcha tiramisu and pudding with cafe lattes, served in a tatami room soundtracked by lazy jazz.

Wife & Husband
ワイフアンドハズバンド

Eclectic cafe with picnic packs just near the Botanical Gardens.

106-6 Shimouchikawara-cho
Koyama Kita-ku

201 7324

Kitaoji

Tues, Wed & Fri 10am–5pm
(variable opening)

JP¥
¥

W
wifeandhusband.jp

Owners Kyoichi and Ikumi Yoshida tell a whimsical tale. It is said that on the first day they spent together, they roasted coffee beans, and they've spent every day since the same way. They want to connect with us 'the way the word husband connects with wife' – words that cannot exist except in combination and they do this in a tiny cafe in the backstreets of Kitaoji. Antiques, found furniture, hanging bicycles, broken clocks and a ceiling of dried flowers warm up the space. We ordered pour-over coffee and some of their delectable honey-cheese toast – something we've been trying to re-create at home ever since. You can takeaway Wife & Husband's appropriately named 'Daughter' blend coffee, or head here for picnic supplies. They sell hampers and you can rent a stool, a straw hat, a parasol and a folding table. With the Botanical Gardens (see p. 176) and the river nearby, who can resist making a day of it?

食事とドリンク

EATING & DRINKING

Kyoto is a city where food is often taken to extravagant heights and culinary heritage is apparent on every plate. Emperors, nobles, artisans, samurai and monks have shaped Kyoto's cuisine over the past 12 centuries. Dishes such as soba, sushi and ramen have been obsessed over and perfected so, no matter your budget, in Kyoto you'll be eating history.

Century-old eateries, speciality restaurants and cute cafes roll up their blinds or slide open their doors to reveal bright and intriguing food displays. Market stalls and street vendors showcase seasonal produce.

Shojin ryori (vegetarian banquets) are eaten in temple grounds and at the historic restaurant Okutan Nanzen-ji (see p. 73). Obanzai (home cooking) lunch sets can be enjoyed at cosy venues like Kokoroya (see p. 52) and Okudohan (see p. 54). Eel is a Kyoto speciality and has been perfected at century-old charmer Kyogoku Kane yo (see p. 61). Kaiseki ryori meals (refined multi-course cuisine) elevate local ingredients to banquets fit for royalty. Italian fare is given a Kyoto twist at Enboca (see p. 57) and Pizzeria Mama (see p. 75).

Kyoto-ites also take their drinks seriously, with most eateries serving up shochu, plum wine sake, lemon sour and whisky highball. In recent times craft beer has become popular, too.

Kyoto Ramen Koji
京都拉麺小路

A sky-high ramen wonderland.

10F Kyoto Station Bldg
Karasuma-dori
Shimogyo-ku

361 4401

Kyoto

Mon–Sun 11am–10pm

JP¥
¥

W
kyoto-ramen-koji.com

There's something a bit 'Jack and the Beanstalk' about heading up into the clouds on the long, slow escalator to this mystical land of ramen above Kyoto station. The famed ramen alley features a range of eateries showcasing the specialties of ramen makers from eight different prefectures. Tuck into flavour-packed Araumado from Osaka, or discover the deep, multi-layered mysteries of the Tokyo Taishoken. Broths aren't just pork – Menya Iroha does a fish-based soy sauce broth, although vegetarians note: it may still arrive with pork slices. Try their famous dish, the addictive Toyama Black. To order food, buy a ticket at one of the vending machines at the front of the store – many machines have an English button. Wash your ramen down with a beer and enjoy liberal helpings of the pickles. It's cheap and fun, and there are plenty of pictures, and even some English, to guide you through the menus on your ramen adventure.

Sobanomi Yoshimura
蕎麦の実 よしむら

A traditional soba house shines among the new builds of Gojo-dori.

420 Matsuyacho
Shimogyo-ku

353 0114

Gojo

Mon–Sun 11am–2.30pm &
5.30–10.30pm

JP¥
¥ ¥

W
arashiyama-yoshimura.com/
soba/sobanomi

You'll find this surprising piece of old Kyoto among the faceless facades on the broad swathe of Gojo-dori. Sobanomi Yoshimura belies its location and delivers one of Kyoto's most atmospheric, inexpensive soba experiences. The warm traditional exterior beckons you into the downstairs room where you can slide into a booth and watch the show; soba being made fresh on the premises – the soba masters work dough into fresh, perfectly chewy noodles. Or head upstairs and order a sake or two, delivered in small squares of luminous glassware. Sip it while looking through the wide windows at the world driving by on busy Gojo-dori. Set menus are perfectly balanced. We opted for the Obanzai Zen, featuring a 'taste of Kyoto': noodles with regional pickles, vegetables and miso and the Tenzaru Zen, which highlights fresh, crunchy tempura. Accompanying dishes including chicken wings and sashimi are equally impressive. In a city revered for its soba, Sobanomi Yoshimura is a standout.

Eating & drinking

Kokoraya
ここら屋

*Local vegetables star in this
friendly, relaxed izakaya.*

---

332 Ebiyacho
Nakagyo-ku

211 3348

Kyoto Shiyakusho-mae

Open Tues–Sun hours vary

JP¥

¥¥

W

kokoraya.moss-co-ltd.com

It's easy to spot this breezy obanzai izakaya
(pub with small plate food) – not far from
Nishiki Market (see p. 63) and Teramachi-dori
(see p. 117) – as the impressive old machiya
(traditional wooden townhouse) always has
an array of brightly coloured vegetables
adorning the exterior. The display hints at
Kokoraya's speciality: home-style, locally
sourced vegetable dishes (although there
are plenty of fish and meat options as well).
The deep woods, latticed doors and windows,
bamboo blinds, posters and blackboard menu
at the front also hint at the messy charm that
continues in the interior. The menu features
obanzai staples: miso, rice, oden, tofu, pickles
and tempura. We ordered a range of delectable
small plates to accompany our sake. The
mackerel sashimi and karaage (fried chicken)
are a perfect pairing with beers and lemon
sours. Local, fresh and laidback, Kokoroya is
perfect for a filling lunch or a boozy night in
the Kyoto backstreets.

Chisou Inaseya
馳走いなせや

Venue with traditional charm serving speciality chicken and sake.

93 Aburaya-Cho Yanagino-
bamba-agaru
Sanjo, Nakagyo-ku

255 7250

Kurasuma Oike

Mon–Sun 11.30am–2.30pm &
5–11pm

JP¥

¥ ¥

W

chisouinaseya.com

Down a tiny lane off Yanaginobamba-dori, you'll discover one of Kyoto's best-kept secrets. Set in a beautiful machiya (traditional wooden townhouse) with old beams, cushions, tatami mats and a Japanese garden, Chisou Inaseya is the kind of place you'll wish was your local. We recommend the lunch menu – Inaseya master Yoshikazu Yokada sources the freshest local ingredients, including standout vegetables and pickles and impeccable Kyoto free-range chicken to make a simple kaiseki bento box. The 'feast Inaseya' lunch consists of seven small dishes cooked in Kyoto style. Make sure you order sake with your meal – we asked our waiter for the best karacuchi (dry) sake and were treated to some of the most delicious local sake we've ever tasted. We each chose a different variety and were poured drinks from gigantic bottles placed on the table, so we could examine the beauty of the labels and memorise the maker. Night-time fare is more occasion dining with expertly prepped kaiseki ryori (refined multi-course cuisine) dining using seasonal ingredients.

Eating & drinking

Okudohan
みます屋 おくどはん

Perfect set meals of simple homestyle cooking with local seasonal ingredients.

318-3 Maryacho
Nakagyo-ku

50 5827 1864

Kyoto Shiyakusho-mae

Mon—Sun 11.30am—3pm &
6pm—10pm

JP¥
¥

Okudohan is like a warm hug and a hearty meal from the Japanese mum you wish you had. Nothing says Kyoto more than obanzai – food that is simply prepared from the heart, seasonal and minimises food waste. Your lunch or dinner set will normally be a series of small plates (there could be as many as 11 or 12) that will include a miso soup, freshly pickled vegetables, rice, tofu, an omelette and a main of meat, seafood or vegetables. Okudohan's cosy, rustic, well-worn old townhouse has booths and counter seats with a view of the chefs and staff in action. Lunch is a friendly, breezy affair, while dinner can get more rambunctious as the drinks begin to flow. There is an extensive blackboard menu outside where you can mentally make your selection. We tried a sashimi lunch set and one where local vegetables were the star, but the fish set or pork and egg sets are a popular choice. Simply perfect.

mumokuteki cafe & foods
ムモクテキ

Simple, sizeable plant-based lunch sets in a rustic cafe.

261 Shikibucho
Nakagyo-ku

213 7733

Sanjo

Thurs—Mon 11.30am–4.30pm

JP¥

¥

W

mumokuteki.com

'Animal free' is the motto at this unpretentious plant-based cafe in the heart of central Kyoto, just a stone's throw from Nishiki Market (see p. 63), and perched above a labyrinthine clothing, homewares and antique store. Lunch sets are flavoursome and feature a satisfying array of dishes, including salads, pickles, miso, rice, fried tofu, okra and konnyaku. The mock-meat dishes will satisfy carnivores and may even win them over from the dark side; a plant-based burger or lotus-root noodles goes perfectly with a healthy juice. Desserts are mostly soy and fruit based; the parfait, vegan tiramisu or honey and tofu cheesecake will hoodwink the sweet toothed into thinking they are eating dairy. A relaxed staff waft in now and again to assure you that no soups use any fish-based stocks. Those with little ones in tow will be happy to see the smiley-faced rice and mock-meat platter – both kawaii (cute) and kenkō (healthy). Afterwards, when you're giddy on tofu and powered by green juice, shop the quirky selections downstairs.

AWOMB Karasuma Honten
アウーム 烏丸本店

Roll your own sushi in this beautifully renovated townhouse.

189 Ubayanagicho
Nakagyo-ku

204 5543

Karasuma

Mon–Sun 12pm–3pm, 6–9pm

JP¥

¥ ¥

W

awomb.com

As soon as you enter through the noren (traditional fabric curtains) and walk down the long corridor, you'll begin to feel AWOMB's Zen-like atmosphere. The room is stunning: superb architecture by Ujita Hiroshi has reworked an old machiya (traditional wooden townhouse) into a minimalist warehouse space (their small but perfect garden was the inspiration for our Japanese garden at home). Awomb's unique take on sushi has seen them garner media attention throughout Japan, and for good reason. Their deconstructed DIY sushi, self-termed teori–zushi ('ori' meaning folding), provides all the base ingredients for you to roll your own creations. Served with elevated obanzai (home cooking) delicacies like pickles, edible flowers and snow pea shoots, your visually impressive sushi ingredients are exquisitely presented on a beautiful dark slate. It's a vivid visual template that has made AWOMB a favourite of locals and tourist alike. Make sure you visit their other branch, AWOMB Nishi-Kiyamachi by the canals – they do a memorable take-out bento lunch box.

Enboca
エンボカ京都

Pizza with locally sourced ingredients in an old textile dyeing store.

406 Ikesucho
Nakagyo-ku

253 0870

Kurasuma Oike

Thurs–Mon 11.30am–2pm & 5–9.30pm

JP¥
¥¥

W
hitosara.com

Riffs, beats and lazy jazz are the soundtrack to Enboca, a pizza eatery housed in a beautiful former shibori (textile dye) shop. Yoshihiro Imai from Philosopher's Path (see p. 19) standout restaurant Monk trained here, so you can expect perfection. Soaring ceilings, wooden beams and low-hanging light bulbs turn this space into a pizza cathedral. The dough is made with sourced well water and then cooked low and slow in a large oven that resembles a pottery kiln, reaching a chewy perfection before being topped with a variety of flavourful and often surprising ingredients. Enboca offers up various delights like lotus root or lily bulb, which you can have as a 'half and half', so you don't miss out on any of the culinary creations. Ham is shaved directly from the bone. We opted for the aforementioned lotus root and also indulged in a moreish quattro formaggi, a honey-drizzled delight. If a beer cocktail takes your fancy, there are three to choose from, including blood orange. The fig or pear sangria is an unmissable home-made tipple and, although it is known for pizza, we would go there for the matcha and white chocolate ganache dessert alone.

Eating & drinking

Apollo Plus
アポロプラス

Local hang with top-notch regional fare and a sake tasting set.

2f, 3f 67 NEOS Sanjo
Masuyacho
Nakagyo-ku

253 6605

Karasuma Oike

Mon–Sun 5pm–12am

JP¥
¥¥

W
apollo-plus.net

Rowdy locals and visitors pack this unpretentious izakaya (pub with small plate food). They come for the atmosphere, but stay for the food, the easy-flowing beer and the cheeky tasting sets of regional sake – three small cups of heaven! You can snack here or go to town ordering everything in sight (and roll out afterwards), depending on your appetite. Our appetites were pretty big, so we had their famous gyoza, tasty yakitori, delicious fresh sashimi and some top-notch (and at times unexpected) oden. The space is a relaxing haven, a repurposed machiya (traditional wooden townhouse) of warm, aged woods, wooden beams, cosy nooks and crannies and dim atmospheric lighting. There are long tables with bench seating if you're feeling communal (which you will be after the sake tasting set). Other menu recommendations include agedashi tofu and potato salad but, ultimately, it's the warm atmosphere that sees locals make this their go-to and visitors want to come back here whenever they are in town.

Cafe Indépendants
アンデパンダン

Underground cafe and bar with a Western-style menu served up with a slice of sedition.

56, 1928 Benkeiishi chô
Nakagyo-ku

255 4312

Sanjo

Mon–Sun 11.30am–12am

JP¥

¥

W

cafe-independants.com

Viva la revolution! Housed in an old socialist meeting place, you can almost smell the ink and hear the talk of revolution at this uber-cool underground cafe and bar. It's a popular hangout for students and intellectuals who want to plot a coup or write their manifesto on the back of a coaster while sipping craft beer. A cafe for the people, they do simple curries, paella (try the squid ink) and revolutionary pastas (mackerel bolognaise anyone?), and a range of tapas at night. There's an extensive list of European beer, which you can quaff in small booths or at bench tables. The walls of exposed brick and white beams seem to barely hold up the building – part of its rustic charm. Check out the side entrance with its dangerously steep stairs and peeling walls glued into place by old posters of Freddie Mercury, cowboy Elvis and pop graphics with revolutionary intent.

Eating & drinking

Kyogoku Kaneyo

京極かねよ

Taste Kyoto culinary history in this century-old eel restaurant.

Eel is a Kyoto speciality, and this restaurant, standing out on a contemporary street, should be on every foodie's to-do list. Before entering, the sweet smell of grilled eel greets you on the street. Red lanterns wave in the breeze and the rustic wooden architecture is enveloped in plumes of smoke. Masters at work can be seen through the front window, preparing eel with deft slices. Kyogoku Kaneyo has been in the business of grilling freshwater eel for over a century and the expertise shows. Slip off your shoes and head inside where the welcome is warm. Follow the winding corridors to rooms with tatami mats, low tables and floor cushions and prepare to experience classic Kyoto cuisine.

Kyogoku has earned a Bib Gourmand in the *Michelin Guide*, and is famous for the simple kinshidon bowl – charcoal grilled eel and omelette with rice. Pair a local sake with the sashimi in a piquant dipping sauce or the tamagoyaki (omelette) with a spicy sweet drizzle. We also heartily recommend the eel with pickled cucumber.

456 Matsugaecho
Nakagyo-ku

221 0669

Sanjo

Thurs–Tues 11.30am–
3.30pm & 5pm–8pm

JP¥
¥ ¥ ¥

W
kyogokukaneyo.co.jp

Nishiki Market
錦市場

Kyoto foodie heaven in an historic covered arcade market.

When it comes to markets, this thin alleyway crammed with stalls, eateries and street vendors is a mouth-watering and eye-popping delight. Nishiki isn't your classic market ramble – it's a concentrated strip that packs a lot into its slim dimensions. It's not known as the 'kitchen of Kyoto' for nothing. You won't get much in the way of Western-style food, and of course that's the charm. It's Japanese cuisine with a strong leaning towards Kyoto specialities, and that means strange seafood grilled on sticks, numerous varieties of tea, sweets, crackers, soft-serve ice-cream (in matcha and black sesame flavours, amongst others) and colourful barrels brimming with all things fermented, both known and unknown. Grab a burdock root or sweet potato stick and wash it down with a yuzu juice. Vintage booze posters hold ramshackle eateries together. Slide in, perch yourself on an upturned milk crate and order up a storm. Join the queue at **Sawawa** for some matcha warabi mochi (powdered sweet jelly).

The market's variety is staggering (and sometimes frightening), but take a chance – you're sure to get an education. Nishiki Market is also a great place to buy Japanese knives; head to **Aritsugu** for a selection that draws chefs and cooks from all corners of the world. Chances are you'll have to sidle your way through an endless sea of people here, but that's what a market is – bustling, loud and crazy – and Nishiki is one of the greats.

Nishikikoji-dori
Nakagyo-ku

Shijo

JP¥
¥

Tues–Sun 9am–5pm

W
kyoto-nishiki.or.jp

231 6828

Eating & drinking

Vegan Ramen UZU

ヴィーガンラーメン ウズ キョウト

*Sit in a dark and mesmerising art installation as you eat award-winning
vegan ramen with locally sourced ingredients.*

On a non-descript street off the general tourist radar, UZU sits quietly in an
architecturally renovated machiya (traditional wooden townhouse). The black-
box exterior with wooden inset door and discreet signage prepares the clientele
for UZU's take on 'concept dining'. Enter the darkened room, where a 'digital
painting' of ever moving and evolving calligraphy brushstrokes generated by
renowned international art collective teamLab, covers the back wall, and is
reflected in the surface of the table, enveloping the space. Other diners are
mere shadows, and the ponderous soundtrack becomes part of the whole
experience (hushed voices are requested here).

Awarded a Bib Gourmand in 2023's *Michelin Guide*, Vegan Ramen
UZU gets the most out of Kyoto's Rausu kelp, shiitake and vegetables,
steeping the stock for twelve hours to deliver a ramen with a potency of taste
that rivals the piquant pork staple. Types of ramen include Kokiake (soy sauce),
Yamabuki (spicy miso) and Tsukemen (sichuan pepper spicy miso). We paired
the mountain herbs ramen with some tasty miyama gomi yuba rolls and a
rose hip and hibiscus kombucha, and finished with some delectable vegan
ice-cream desserts.

146 Umenokicho
Nakagyo-ku

80 7603 6106

Jingu-Marutamachi

Thurs–Sun 11.30am–
2.30pm & 6pm–9pm

JP¥
¥¥

W
vegan-uzu.com/pages/
uzu-kyoto

Eating & drinking

Cafe Bibliotec Hello
カフェ ビブリオティック ハロー！

Plant therapy, a cosy office, library and cafe in the heart of the action.

---

650 Nijo-dori, Seimei-cho
Nakagyo-ku

231 8625

Kyoto Shiyakusho-mae

Mon–Sun 11.30am–12am

JP¥
¥

W
cafe-hello.jp

You may be forgiven for thinking you are walking towards an urban jungle, not a cafe, on your first trip to Cafe Bibliotec Hello. Inside, the potted plants, palms, ferns and even a tree give the impression of a Victorian-era greenhouse, albeit one with mid-century furniture and ceramics. A popular hangout for locals and visitors alike, this cafe's towering bookcases, cosy chairs and chill vibes instantly make you feel welcome. Wooden beams fringe the walkway that divides the two floors, with both levels housing small libraries that boast covetable collections of design books. Locals sit at bench tables and tip tap on laptops or scribble in journals while sipping coffee, making the cafe feel like it's part writer's retreat. Head in for lunch or dinner (the chicken curry hits the spot) or order a sandwich and munch along in time to the soundtrack of nostalgic jazz and pop. They serve olives with your drinks here, cementing the '60s vibe, and the beer and plum wine are inexpensive. It all makes for a comfy day hangout or super cool night bar.

Kushikura
串くら

Perfect yakitori in an old kimono store.

584 Hiiragicho
Nakagyo-ku

213 2211

Karasuma Oike

Mon–Sun 11.30am–2.30pm &
5–9.30pm

JP¥
¥ ¥

W
kushikura.jp

A century of history and good times set the scene at Kushikura, an authentic yakitori restaurant housed in an old kimono store. The kimono must have been precious indeed, as the setting is stunning: boasting tatami mats, delicate shoji screens and circular windows looking onto a beautiful tsuboniwa (small Japanese garden). Foodies eager to learn skills from the masters should take a seat at the counter where you can watch the chefs in action. But usually you'll be served in hidden rooms that lead from a winding corridor on horigotatusu tables – low to the ground but with a recessed area for your legs. Yakitori skewers and grilled chicken dishes are served with miso, rice and premium pickles. They use an expertly chosen grade of chicken and local seasonal vegetables are chargrilled to perfection (vegetable-only skewers can be made on request). When we were here, the lunch special was hitsumabushi – quarters of chicken paired with rice, raw egg and dashi stock. Make like a local and try the kyo-age: turnip leaves wrapped around fried tofu, and wash it down with a fushimi sake selection. Oishii!

Eating & drinking

Honke Owariya Main Branch

本家尾張屋 本店

One of Japan's oldest restaurants serving perfect soba since 1465.

---

322 Niomontsukinukecho
Nakagyo-ku

231 3446

Kurasuma Oike

Mon–Sun 11am–7pm

JP¥

¥ ¥

W

honke-owariya.co.jp/en

People talk about visiting ancient temples, but have you ever eaten at a restaurant that's more than 500 years old? When, after a hard day of praying and meditating, monks in ancient Kyoto needed to refuel, Honke Owariya supplied the soba. Step through the noren (traditional fabric curtains) into the small courtyard, where a tranquil Japanese garden sets the scene. Inside is an unmissable two-storey house from feudal times ... slip into one of the corner tables or scissor yourself down onto a tatami mat and sip sake. The houri soba set special is a pillar of boxes featuring fresh, chewy soba noodles, prawn tempura and an assortment of vegetables. Lucky for us there's an English menu to save us learning a 500-year-old dialect. This is the food of the monks and it has stood the test of time without elevating the prices. Don't forget to grab one of their sweet rice cakes on the way out. Honke Owariya started out as a confectioner – so the sweets are older than the soba!

Gion Mametora

祇をん 豆寅

Jewel-like boxed sushi lunch sets.

570-235 Gionmachi
Minamigawa
Higashiyama-ku

532 3955

Gion-Shijo

Mon–Sun 11.30am–2pm &
5–9pm

JP¥

¥ ¥ ¥

W

kiwa-group.co.jp/mametora_
gion/

Kyoto food memories are definitely made of this. Mametora serves a world-famous version of mamezushi – Kyoto's unique style of sushi. Often referred to as Maiko sushi, the size and shape is made to perfectly fit the 'button-shaped' mouths of the apprentice geisha. Downstairs, small private rooms spill off a lantern-lit hallway. Upstairs, the immaculate room is the epitome of classic beauty, complete with traditional art and ikebana (the art of flower arranging). The well-priced five-course set lunch gives you a glimpse of the majesty of kaiseki ryori (refined multi-course cuisine), a small plate feast that builds up to the *ooh* and *aah* moment of the mamezushi set. The special wooden boxes feature an assortment of sushi, bamboo shoots and pickled tuna, so beautifully arranged you feel like you are being presented with a tray of gems. It's a study in style and beauty, and the clientele are dressed accordingly.

Eating & drinking

Tempura Endo Yasaka

天ぷら圓堂　八坂本店

One of the most highly regarded tempura restaurants in the world.

Tempura Endo sits quietly on Yasaka-dori, prime Kyoto real estate which runs up to the five-tiered pagoda of Hokan-ji and basks in the protective glow of Kennin-ji temple (see p. 185). It is housed in a stunning century-old sukiyaki zukuri–style teahouse, once a performance space for geisha and maiko (apprentice geisha), and prices match the surrounds – dinner is certainly an indulgence. Lunchtime sets, however, are a Kyoto secret and a real bargain for this memorable experience. Sit at the counter and watch the masters at work – each delicate piece of tempura will be placed before you like a precious gift. Their speciality corn tempura is a standout, so are the sea urchin wrapped in dried seaweed, bracken, various mushrooms, freshwater fish and seasonal veggies which can all be lightly sprinkled with matcha or yuzu salt or dunked in delicious dipping sauce.

You can stalk the Tempura Endo website from the time you book to the time you arrive and put together your fantasy menu. All allergies and food intolerances can be catered for when booking in advance. Their 'no children under 12' policy might seem harsh, but it sets a gently refined air which will appeal to some. If you'd like to try their cuisine and can't get a booking, contact Endo in advance and pick up some boxed tempura rice rolls to take away.

📍 566 Komatsu-cho Higashiyama-ku	🚋 Kiyomizu-Gojo	JP¥ ¥¥¥
📞 551 1488	🕑 Mon–Fri 11.30am–3pm & 7–10pm	W gion-endo.com

Eating & drinking

Okutan Nanzen-ji

奥丹 南禅寺店

Longstanding tofu restaurant that once served the monks of Nanzen-ji.

Just across from the Nanzen-ji temple grounds (see p. 172), in the tranquil backstreets that lead to the Philosopher's Path (see p. 19), you'll find Okutan Nanzen-ji, set in a modest yet beautiful building, girded by wood and bamboo, with a striking thatched roof. As the oldest boiled tofu restaurant in Kyoto, dating back over 370 years, Okutan once made purifying, fortifying meals for the monks of Nanzen-ji. With such an extensive history, and secret family recipes passed down through the years, plant-based eaters and carnivores alike are in for a feast for the senses.

You'll be served in small rooms on low tables seated on zabuton cushions. Glass shoji sliding doors and windows overlook a delightful garden. They only serve one meal: the boiled tofu set. The tofu is boiled in a clay pot on your table, and extras include sesame goma-dofu, vegetable tempura, fried tofu on a skewer (with miso), soup and pickles. Tofu afficionados can select different tofus from different regions at varying price points. The area and restaurant are popular, so turn up at opening time and put your name on the list outside to avoid disappointment!

86-30 Nanzenji
Fukuchicho
Sakyo-ku

771 8709

Keage

Open Fri–Wed
11am–2pm

JP¥
¥¥¥

Eating & drinking

Omen
おめん

*Simple, perfect udon lunch
sets near the Silver Temple.*

74 Ishibashi-cho
Jodo-ji, Sakyo-ku

771 8994

Ginkakuji mae

Mon–Sun 11am–9pm

JP¥

¥¥

W

omen.co.jp

If you are contemplating life and the universe along the Philosopher's Path (see p. 19) or stepping out of Ginkaku-ji (Silver Temple), Omen is nearby to fill the void. It's good to know you don't need to rush here, as Omen doesn't adhere to Kyoto's strict opening and closing lunch hours. You'll know you've arrived when you see the hiragana sign お めん, noren (traditional fabric curtains) and queue of foodies. Try one of the set meals from the English menu. A perfect choice for those with a plant-based diet, the Omen Udon set is a display of seasonal vegetables, pickles, toasted sesame seeds and a mountainous pile of daikon (a type of radish) arranged beautifully on a long plate. The kamo (duck) udon is a standout with its umami dashi broth and delicately cooked meat. Yes, it's a popular place, and you'll likely have to queue, but omen means *honourable noodle*, and you'll be eating some of Kyoto's best udon.

Pizzeria Mama

A contemporary pizza and pasta eatery away from the Arashiyama crowds.

1-5 Arashiyama
Nishiichikawacho
Nishikyo-ku

366 3885

Arashiyama (Hankyu line)

Mon–Sun 11am–9pm

JP¥

¥¥

W

mama-arashiyama.jp

On the quieter backstreets on the Hankyu Arashiyama station side of the Togetsu-kyo Bridge, large white noren (traditional fabric curtains) wave you into a bright, contemporary space, where you'll find the destination hotel of Arashiyama House MAMA and Pizzeria MAMA. An old building reimagined by DAY Inc and run by Akihiko Watanabe, the impressive restaurant room makes a feature of the original vaulted wooden ceiling and large windows that gaze out onto beautiful gardens. The décor is sparse – stark, potted trees and a polished concrete floor are designed so that the diners can 'complete the space'. Pizza sets come with soup and salad and the pizza base is perfectly crispy meets chewy wood-fired heaven. Toppings include sardines, mackerels and cheese and honey and flavours are piquant. Other dishes include pork roast and various pasta dishes. This is a popular place enjoyed by a stylish set, families and gourmands. If you are staying at the hotel, book a table when you check in. Visitors can try their luck on the day, but wait times can extend to two hours.

Eating & drinking

Arashiyama Yoshimura
嵐山よしむら

Come for the food, stay for the view.

3 Sagatenryuji Susukinobabacho
Ukyo-ku

863 5700

Arashiyama

Mon–Sun 11am–4pm

JP¥

¥ ¥

W

yoshimura-gr.com/arashiyama

This Arashiyama restaurant, sister to Gojo-dori's Sobanomi Yoshimura (see p. 51), has a major drawcard – the perfect 180-degree corner view that takes in the Togetsu-kyo Bridge, the flowing Katsura River and whatever stunning seasonal foliage or snowy vista happens to be peacocking on Mount Arashiyama. The 'Arashiyama Villa' setting is a charmer too – a haven of wooden beams and bamboo that once played host to artists Kawamura Manshu, Kitaoji Rosanjin and Yokoyama Taikan. The food was always going to play second fiddle to the view, but simple soba noodle dishes featuring locally sourced buckwheat are a fine accompaniment and crafted by over 30 artisan buckwheat noodle makers, who still grind their flour with stone mills. The a la carte tempura selection is recommended so you can try a range of freshly made tempura. Of course, it's ridiculously popular, and they don't take bookings, so appear magically at opening time and queue to put your name down.

Sarasa Nishijin
さらさ西陣

*A beautiful old bathhouse
is transformed into a
neighbourhood cafe.*

11-1 Higashi Fujinomori-cho
Murasakino, Kita-ku

432 5075

Kuramaguchi

Mon–Sun 12–11pm

JP¥

¥

W

sarasan2.exblog.jp

In times gone by, people came to relax and soak away their cares at this bathhouse. Now converted into one of our favourite cafes, you can still come here to relax, but it's probably best to keep your clothes on. Take in the amazing frontage. This is one of the finest examples of a beautiful old building that has been repurposed and contemporised in North Kyoto. The majestic gabled roof and the highly decorative tiles slightly obscured by rows of bicycles – it's simply picturesque. Head inside and slide into a booth, admiring the 80-year-old patterned wall tiles that give the space an almost Moroccan look. Original walls, disintegrating and half knocked down, partition the room and local club fliers and various books and posters give it a definite local drop-in centre vibe. It's spacious for a Kyoto cafe, so make yourself at home and order up an omelette or pizza, and a Clamp coffee (see p. 42) – same owners, same quality coffee. Those who loved the bathhouse might lament its loss, but cafe fans have a new go-to.

Eating & drinking

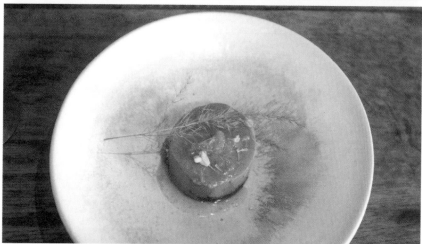

Stardust

スターダスト

Elegant and enigmatic vegan cafe in Kyoto's peaceful north.

Time moves differently at Stardust. Host Kana floats in and out of the rooms, radiating universal energy. Nature punctuates the rustic space – balls of moss form on concrete, and tendrils of greenery hang from the ceiling. Flora and fauna displays and crystals and brass candle holders adorn the mismatched wooden tables and chairs.

Stardust is part cafe and part 'beautiful things'. Book in advance for the cafe, as their seasonal vegan lunch is made in limited quantities. Pair it with an organic wine or whimsically presented seasonal fruit juice, which comes in Osaka's Ricordo glassware, and follow up with one of their delicious 'raw sweets', presented on exquisite crockery like tiny pieces of art adorned with little wisps of nature. The 'beautiful things' come in the form of artfully curated ceramics, textiles, jewellery and the wafting elegance of Cosmic Wonder's designer clothing. Books, coffee beans and more are all chosen here because they light up this little corner of the universe.

41 Shichiku Shimotakedonocho Kita-ku	Kitaoji	JP¥ ¥¥
286 7296	Mon–Sun 11am–6pm	W stardustkyoto.com

牛です。

ロース
ステーキ重
二二〇円

煮付き

穴子の

おばんざい・みそ汁・佃煮付き

タラコあんが
絶妙にマッチ‼

鶏天とだし巻玉子
タラコあんかけ丼

汁・佃煮付き

九五〇

の西京焼と
出汁巻玉子膳
一八〇円

北海道産ゆめぴりか米の白飯
みそ汁・おばんざい・佃煮
付き

お肉が
toroです。

豚の角煮御膳
二九〇円

北海道産ゆめぴりか米
みそ汁・おばんざい付き

定番のカツとじ
ごくごはんならではの
美味しさを‼

北海道産ゆめぴりか米の白飯

9種重のおばんざい
食後のデザート,ドリング

ごっこ
町御膳
一二五〇円

おばんざい
甘味も入

熱々‼
カツとじ
御膳
二〇〇円

月〜金曜日(平日)

お茶と御菓子

TEA & SWEETS

The earliest records of tea or cha 茶 in Japan date back to the 8th century when tea was introduced from China. In the 15th century, early pioneers of the tea ceremony, Zen Buddhist monks, elevated it to ceremonial status using principles of wabi-sabi (perfection in imperfection), chadō ('the way of tea', known as the tea ceremony) is one of the three classical refined arts in Japan. Kyoto and its neighbour Uji (see p. 217), are among the oldest and most notable tea producing regions in Japan. The smell of freshly roasted green tea floats through Kyoto's streets. You'll also find some of Japan's historic, original teahouses on display in specific Kyoto gardens.

Of course, you can't have tea without wagashi (Japanese sweets), small gem-like delights in seasonal shapes and colours. Toraya (see p. 90) has been making sweets since the early 16th century, and you can try dango (rice flour) dumplings on skewers drizzled with sweet miso at Kazariya (see p. 99). Malebranche (see p. 147) do a delicious cha-no-ka (longue du chat), which goes perfectly with tea. Don't miss a Kyoto special, the elaborate parfait in a towering glass filled with matcha sponge, mochi (sweet rice cakes), jelly and ice-cream, at Shichijo Kanshundo (see p. 95), Saryo Suisen (see p. 87), and Tsuji Rihei Honten (see p. 217). Head into the forest for a matcha affogato at Mo-an (see p. 96), and don't miss Horaido (see p. 117), an historic tea store and the birthplace of genmaicha.

Ma
間

A Kyoto slow tea experience that combines deep tradition with inventive presentation.

Time seems to move differently at Ma. In the shadow of To-ji temple's magnificent pagoda (see p. 154), you'll find a quiet street leading to a secret teahouse. White noren (traditional fabric curtains) beckon you into a space peppered with antiques and filled with gentle music and an air of deep tranquility. Wait until it is your turn, and then head further in where you'll find a room of beautiful dark woods, windows that filter diffused, almost spiritual light and a towering ceiling. Blinds and shoji screens decorate one wall, while quirky statues and art (including a sword in a stone and a silver pegasus) lend the space a playful air. Tea tasting sets allow you to try a selection of quality Japanese and Chinese tea. We chose the thick matcha, a dense green tea with a memorably intense flavour that can be softened with the addition of hot water. Find a seat by the gently steaming kettle and watch the ceremony unfold. Tea comes paired with perfectly formed, jewel-like wagashi (Japanese sweets).

A small store and gallery sells tea in sachets (you can mix and match box sets of tea) and the cafe's inventive ceramics.

59 Nishikujo Hieijocho
Minami-ku

748 6198

Toji

Thurs–Mon 11am–5pm

JP¥
¥¥

W
tea.oma.jp

Tea & sweets

Kaikado Cafe
カイカドウカフェ

Stunning century-old shop and cafe selling wabi-sabi (perfection in imperfection) tea canisters.

84-1 Umeminatocho
Shimogyo-ku

351 5788

Shichijo

Mon–Sun 12pm–6pm

JP¥
¥ ¥

W
kaikado.jp

Kaikado are famous for their perfectly turned and expertly-crafted tin plate chazutsu (Japanese tea canisters). The Kaikado family of master craftsmen has worked for over 100 years and through six generations, to craft a true Kyoto design classic. The cafe, housed in a repurposed 1927 building, is industrial chic – exposed brick with large sliding windows of steel and glass, hanging lamps, stark and minimalist lines and the beautiful chazutsu on display in big blonde-wood cabinets. While we contemplated making our long-desired purchase, we relaxed with a perfectly made tea and a cheeky cheesecake shaped just like the canisters. Don't miss the gallery/showroom space upstairs, a masterclass in wabi-sabi (perfection in imperfection) interior styling and patinated product; staff will talk you through the ageing process of copper, tin and brass, which improves the materials in both character and richness. Nearby, a small, hidden Kaikado store has their full product range (84-1 Umeminato-cho, Shimogyo-ku).

Saryo Suisen
茶寮翠泉

Afternoon rendezvous for refined tea paired with immoral desserts.

521 Inaricho
Shimogyo-ku

278 0111

Shijo

Mon–Sun 10.30am–6pm

JP¥

¥ ¥

W

saryo-suisen.com

Sinful, yet sophisticated, grown-up, yet playfully indulgent, Saryo Suisen is a famous, stylish old-school cafe that does all the classics impeccably well. You could order a green tea with a tiny, precious wagashi (Japanese sweet), but this is no time to be a puritan – you've come here for an over-the-top dessert. Sweets range from Japanese classics to Western-style desserts, albeit with their own twist. The warabimochi (bracken starch jelly) is outrageous, a 'frozen moment' spilling over the side of a tall glass like a wayward science experiment, or try the off-kilter, voluminous matcha Mont Blanc. The roll cake is a good choice, but the coup de grâce is the towering matcha parfait: the 1950s-style sundae with sponge, matcha ice-cream, red beans, glutinous rice balls, chiffon cake and dusted jelly is the queen of Kyoto desserts. Pair with a classic whisked matcha or a playful matcha latte topped with kawaii (cute) latte art. It's perfect for sharing and you'll see lunching ladies and grown men (who should know better) doing just that.

Tea & sweets

Rau
ラウ

Sculptural desserts made from nature.

3F 1-318-6 Good Nature Station
Inaricho Shimogyo-ku

352 3724

Kyoto-Kawaramachi

Mon–Sun 10am–7pm

JP¥
¥¥

W
rau-kyoto.com

Master patisserie chef Yusuke Matsushita and chocolate chef par excellence Sachiyo Takagi left jobs in highly regarded restaurants to craft desserts of artistic, sculptural beauty at **Good Nature Station** (a hotel and nature foods and products department store). Fruit and vegetable extracts are molded into opulent treasures that you would be more than happy to find on the menu of a Michelin starred restaurant. Perfect to elevate a picnic feast, you can takeaway from the downstairs outlet. If you prefer, dine in upstairs at Rau with a local crowd who come to pair the opulent desserts with tea. Rau presents a dazzling range of colours and shapes, sweets that maximise the flavour palate and forms of plants that are displayed like contemporary works of art on a voluptuously curved counter. We chose 'Yama,' shaped like a snowcapped mountain topped with fluffy clouds, featuring flavours of chestnut, chestnut praline, cassis and white chocolate, and 'Bin', subtitled 'a picnic on a sunny day,' featuring wild strawberries, earl grey mousse and wild rose.

Umezono Café & Gallery
うめぞの カフェアンドギャラリー

Fluffy matcha pancakes in a cosy urban space.

180 Fudocho
Nakagyo-ku

245 0577

Kurasuma

Mon–Sun 11.30am–7pm

JP¥

¥ ¥

W

umezono-kyoto.com

A cafe style (and more relaxed version) of the specialist yokan (jellied red bean paste sweet) shop of Umezono Sabo (see p. 97) in Kyoto's north, Umezono Café & Gallery serves a mix of Japanese and Western-style sweets, drinks and small plates. They specialise in 'an' (red bean paste), and you can try it in a variety of delicious guises. 'An'-mitsu dates back to the Meiji period (1868–1912) and is a popular sweet consisting of red bean, mochi (sweet rice cake) dumplings and agar jelly, often accompanied by fruit. We ordered the lavish matcha sponge parfait, and their famous fluffy matcha pancakes topped with plenty of mildly sweet red bean. On hot days, the towering kakigori (shaved-ice dessert) is the perfect cool-down sweet. 'An'-based drinks or hot or iced coffee (try a red-bean latte) are the perfect accompaniment. Make sure to look around the tiny gallery selling local crafts too.

Tea & sweets

Toraya
とらや

Historic wagashi brand housed in an architectural cafe.

---

415 Hirohashidonocho
Kamigyo-ku

441 3111

Imadegawa

Tues–Sun 9am–6pm

JP¥

¥ ¥

W

toraya-group.co.jp/english

If you could package Kyoto, it would look like a Toraya wagashi (Japanese sweet). Toraya has been making exquisite wagashi since the 1600s. Now in their 17th generation, this amazing family has upheld the principles of reflecting nature and the seasons in their beautiful creations made from 'an' (red bean paste). Toraya engage the five senses and just seeing these elegant sweets will make you want to touch, taste and smell them – and then you'll hear the sound of joy they evoke in people, so that's the five senses covered. A longstanding affinity with nature and simplicity extends to the tearoom, a contemporary and architecturally designed marvel, with an arched wooden roof, water features, a relaxing outdoor zone overlooking Japanese gardens and torii gates, and an adjoining gallery showing beautifully curated exhibitions. Toraya is where art and sweets meet, and you may want to frame the elegantly designed, iconic packaging.

Hitsuji
ひつじ

Healthy donuts with inventive flavours.

335 Oicho
Nakagyo-ku

221 6534

Marutamach

Thurs–Sat 10am–7pm

JP¥
¥

Tiny take-out donut cafe Hitsuji is spoken about in whispers. The rustic texture, artisan look and feel and surprising flavour combinations make their donuts some of the finest you'll find in Japan, and bring locals coming back again and again. The motto here is healthy and natural. The donuts are made from natural yeast and sprouted rice, which gives rise to the phrase 'breathing donuts'. Sweetened with fine Japanese sugar and treated with special care when rising the dough, these donuts will be among the lightest, fluffiest treats you've tasted. Choose from flavours displayed in English, such as the inventive and tantalising black tea and cream cheese, sweet potato and black sesame, or pumpkin with chestnut and coconut – and all at a price point that will extend your already broad smile. Or, join hordes of locals and get one of their caramel rusks. Opening days are limited but join the queue and pick up some delicacies to take on a picnic in the gardens – if they make it that far ...

Tea & sweets

Yugen

ユウゲン

A refined, cutting-edge take on the traditional tearoom.

Yugen is a sophisticated and contemporary tea experience that manages to feel impossibly elegant but down to earth and friendly at the same time. While at pains to point out that they are a traditional tea shop, Yugen will nonetheless leave you in no doubt that this is new Kyoto at its finest. The simple frontage of Yugen will surprise you and inside you'll find that the architecture of the room is as precise as a tea ceremony – brushed concrete and steel are softened by light woods. Locals come here for impeccably sourced tea that is selected with intense scrutiny from plantations in the nearby tea capital of Uji (see p. 216), and poured with deft precision and reverential intensity. Your tea comes with a choice of sweets and we opted for a simple yet elegant peach parfait and a delicate wagashi (Japanese sweet), beautifully presented and expertly paired with the subtle, exquisite tea.

You can buy a selection of refined ceramics, tableware and tea-making tools from the online store too. Tea aficionados will find Yugen an intriguing counterpoint, and yet at the same time a present-day reflection, to the famous, intricate Kyoto tea rituals.

146 Kameyacho
Nakagyo-ku

708 7770

Marutamachi

Mon–Sun 11am–6pm

JP¥

¥ ¥

W

yugen-kyoto.com

Tea & sweets

Book & Café Kotoba no Haoto
古書と茶房 ことばのはおと

This retro-themed cafe is the cat's whiskers.

12-1 Tenjin Kitamachi
Kamigyo-ku

414 2050

Kuramaguchi

Thurs–Sun 11.30am–6pm

JP¥
¥¥

W
kotobanohaoto.net

Only in Japan will you find a cat-themed dessert house, and only in Kyoto will you find it in a beautiful machiya (traditional wooden townhouse). Follow the cat on the noren (traditional fabric curtains) as it beckons you inside. Take a seat – you might be waiting a while, but this is an experience you simply cannot find anywhere else. You'll be ushered into a quiet room with cute couples on dates and friends catching up over a matcha latte or a rice plate lunch. There's plenty of 'cattitude' in the room. Cheeky cat ceramics and maneki-neko (lucky cat) figurines pop out of bookcases as quiet music drifts from an '80s sound system. You can draw cats in books provided, but it's all passing time while you wait for dessert – the super-cute cat parfait, an ice-cream cat-shaped head bobbing out of a sundae glass crammed with biscuits and jelly. In a country of kawaii (cute), this is a high point and, yet, somehow the blend of the traditional room and the cuteness overload is quintessential modern Kyoto.

Shichijo Kanshundo
七条甘春堂

Old-world Kyoto comes to life in this memorable cafe and shop.

11-1 Murasakinohigashifujino-mori-cho
Kita-ku

432 5088

Shichijo

Mon–Sun 11.30am–7pm

JP¥
¥ ¥

W
7jyo-kansyundo.co.jp

Perched amongst the delights of South Higashiyama is a mystical sweet shop and cafe set in a stunning building that dates back to 1865. Stepping in is like walking through a door to another time and place – the service, the ambience, the menu – everything conspires to make you drift back to simpler, gentler days. The Shasa (shaza-kissa) tearoom features tatami mat rooms with shoji screens opening out on to a delightful garden. Order some seasonal wagashi (Japanese sweets) – at times there are 100 to choose from, all beautifully shaped to represent the sakura (cherry blossom) bloom or reddening maple leaves. The popular pick is the o-cha-mochi which cuts through the astringency of the green tea with a gentle sweetness. We chose a matcha tea with a wobbly mound of matcha flavoured jelly and the parfait, a more traditional take on the famous Kyoto dessert, with red bean and sweet potato forming a slightly less sweet but totally delicious dessert. The shop features beautifully packaged and artfully shaped sweets. Note: they also run confectionery classes.

Tea & sweets

Mo-An
茂庵

*A teahouse in a treehouse –
this is enchanted Kyoto at
its best.*

8 Yoshidakaguraokacho
Sakyo-ku

761 2100

Ginkakuji mae

Mon–Fri 12pm–4.30pm

JP¥
¥ ¥

W
mo-an.com

You'll have to go deep into the forest to find
this teahouse in a treehouse, but once the
trek is over, you'll be rewarded with an almost
fairytale-like experience. Dreamily beautiful,
this two-storey machiya (traditional wooden
townhouse) will quickly put you under its
spell. Climb the stairs, breathe in the woody
scent and note the dark greens of the trees.
There's no wicked witch here, but you might
see Hansel and Gretel tucking into the matcha
affogato, a take on the Italian classic. The
twist here is that you'll be pouring green tea
instead of coffee – we don't have to tell you
to eat it quickly before the ice-cream melts
into a heavenly gooey mess. While away the
afternoon with a book at this quiet woodland
retreat, or bring a friend, but remember
to speak at a whisper; this is a place of
contemplation. If you're having trouble finding
your way out of the forest, just follow Hansel
and Gretel's breadcrumbs.

Umezono Sabo
うめぞの茶房

Handmade wagashi in a beautiful space on a quiet northern street.

11-1 Murasakinohigashifujino-mori-cho
Kita-ku

432 5088

Kuramaguchi

Mon–Sun 11.30am-7pm

JP¥

¥¥

W

umezono-kyoto.com

Umezono is a wagashi (Japanese sweet) store operating on another plane. An unassuming entryway with a tiny bonsai and a blackboard with minimal kanji is a portal to a transcendent north Kyoto experience. Inside, the downstairs counter sells ten different varieties of delectable wagashi, perched on tiny white pedestals like works of art. For an unforgettable experience, climb the steep stairs and head into a room of brushed walls, exposed original beams and warm, dark wood furniture. This is an immaculate setting for perfectly blended tea, whisked matcha or homemade fruit drink, as well as some of the finest cakes we've ever had. Their philosophy is to add a European influence to the sweets, but the wormwood with bean jam, white bean with almonds and mugwort soy flour with almonds, all topped with lemon cream and roasted tea icing are, to us, uniquely Japanese. Come here for a contemporary, chic update of wagashi, in what is a perfect example of the city's inventive north.

Tea & sweets

Kazariya

あぶり餅 本家 根元 かざりや

A northern Shinto shrine hides a sweet destination.

Does the idea of perfectly grilled, skewered dumplings in sweet white miso sauce served in serene surrounds under the benevolent gaze of a Shinto shrine appeal? Of course it does! Exit east of Imamiya Jinja shrine (not far from the famed Daitoku-ji complex) where you'll find yourself on a cobbled path flanked by two impressive 17th-century houses. Kazariya has perfected aburi-mochi – sweet roasted glutinous rice cakes, skewered and grilled, lathered in the aforementioned sweet sauce and served with fresh tea. It features tatami mats, circular windows, shoji screens and low lighting infusing warm woods with an other-wordly charm. You can watch the sweet dumplings being grilled and lathered at the front of the store before tucking in – the texture is chewy and the taste is sweet with an irresistible sharpness. The Yasurai Matsuri Festival takes place around here and the aburi-mochi are an important part of the festivities, so you know they going to be good. As an added bonus aburi-mochi are said to bring good luck, driving away evil spirits (and hunger).

Across the road from Kazariya is another confectionery shop **Ichimonjiya Wasuke**, considered the oldest shop in Japan, established in the year 1000 CE, and now in its 25th generation of family ownership.

96 Murasakino
Imamiyacho
Kita-ku

491 9402

Kitaoji

Mon–Tues & Thurs–Sun
10am–5pm

JP¥
¥

Tea & sweets

Gelato Koki
Single
Double (w)

老舗・ヴィンテージと専門店

ARTISAN SHOPPING

As soon as we set foot in Kyoto Station, we sense something waiting in the corner of a dusty vintage shop or on the shelf of an artisan store. Kyoto shopping is an inspiring hunt and gather of both the time-worn and precious, and the newly crafted, innovative and exquisite. Everyday objects are imbued with Kyoto's enchanting power – ceramics, textiles, ikebana vases, artisan knives, baskets, lacquerware, stationery, kimono and geta (wooden sandals). Antiques are rediscovered and repurposed at SOWGEN (see p. 113). The finest incense can be found at longstanding stores like Kyukyodo (see p. 143) and exquisite lacquerware at Zohiko (see p. 118), who have been perfecting their trade for over 400 years. Must-have homewares can be sourced at Ouchi (see p. 130), Essence Kyoto (see p. 129) and Lader (see p. 123). Traditional stores sit next to cutting-edge fashion houses and homewares stores on Teramachi-dori, Rokkaku-dori and Sanjo-dori, while contemporary shopping can be found on busy Shijo-dori.

Our house is populated by many things that were bought while shopping in Kyoto, and memories of trips past sit on shelves and in cabinets – precious items that make our home feel like a tiny piece of Kyoto is always with us.

Roastery Daughter/Gallery Son
ロースタリー ドーター/ギャラリー サン

*A pilgrimage for people
keen to buy quality beans
and grinds, expertly
sourced and freshly roasted.*

22 Kamayacho
Shimogyo-ku

203 2767

Kyoto

Tues–Wed & Fri–Sun
12pm–6.30pm

JP¥
¥¥

W
wifeandhusband.jp

North Kyoto's Wife & Husband (see p. 45) has come to warm the heart of Kyoto's south. Roastery Daughter/Gallery Son sees the couple inventing metaphorical children to set up a coffee mecca with an artistic twist. The 1950's building is a real find, look for the big retro 'coffee' sign that adorns the charming frontage. Inside, you'll find a hive of activity, frenetically buzzing around an array of coffee roasting and grinding machines. You can't get a coffee here, but this place is all about helping you to become your own barista by selecting and purchasing your own beans and grinds. Upstairs you'll find the 'gallery' part of the equation, a small trinket shop featuring vintage and nostalgic ephemera, such as tags, labels, shoes and rustic furniture with a French flair. The gallery also has small showings of beautifully curated and precious art, atelier and illustration. It is intimate, surprising, nostalgic and coloured by a sense of fun – like the 100 thermoses and picnic tools exhibition.

Utsuwa Monotsuki
うつわ ものつき

Off-the-grid ceramics made by some of the most creative artisan potters in Kyoto.

25 Nishikazariyacho
Shimogyo-ku

5359 4425

Gojo

Fri–Wed 11am–7pm

JP¥
¥¥

W
monotsuki.com

Head deep into the bowels of the MCEI building to find this sliver of a room, somewhere between an exhibition space and a store, featuring rustic wooden shelves and tables showcasing some of the most covetable local ceramics. Utsuwa translates roughly as vessel, and you'll find all kinds of cups, plates, dishes and bowls molded out of clay, complete with rough-hewn edges and wonderful quirks and blemishes. The vessels exhibit a simple elegance, unadorned so that the integral beauty is enhanced. Peruse the selection as if you are in a gallery but unlike an art space, you can buy the treasured items at a price point that belies the craftsmanship. Note: After walking out with your prized purchases, don't forget to stop at **Maruni** cafe (the cafe for Marni Atelier) where they elevate the street food taiyaki (a fish-shaped pastry) to the next level.

D&Department
ディアンドデパートメント

A contemporary design store on temple grounds.

If you've ever wanted to worship at a shrine of design, here's your chance.
A showcase for D&Department's perfectly curated selection is housed in a
beautiful building on the grounds of Bukko-ji, a Zen temple that dates back to
1324 CE. The temple has a dark and interesting past featuring bandits, murders
and untimely deaths. There is little evidence of this subversive plotline today,
however. Instead, in a collaboration with the Kyoto School of Art and Design
and the Shin-Buddhism Bukko-ji Temple faction, D&Department creates a
striking outlet for the contemporary aesthetic of their designer homewares.
Meditate upon the simple beauty of the objects – a mix of stationery, kitchenalia,
textiles, food products and more – it's the best of regional Japan brought
together under one ancient roof. Many of these products are unique to Kyoto,
such as utensils and knives made by local artisans. With affordable price points,
you won't leave empty handed.

Hungry? The teishoku and shokudo (simple homestyle lunch and dinner
sets) eatery, **d Shokudo**, is set up in a tatami room on the temple grounds where
the monks used to make and prepare tea. It's now the spiritual home of a lunch
set that showcases light seasonal vegetable dishes with rice and soup, coffee
and dessert. In the warmer months, the sliding doors of the cafeteria are opened
up, giving you an open air view of the temple.

📍 397 Shinkaicho Shimogyo-ku	🚃 Shijo	JP¥ ¥ ¥
📞 343 3217	🕐 Mon–Fri 11am–6pm, Sat–Sun 11am–8pm	W d-department.com/jp/ shop/kyoto

Artisan shopping

kitone
木と根

*Bespoke treasures fill
this small but perfectly
formed store.*

---

589 Torocho
Shimogyu-ku

352 2428

Gojo

Tues–Sat 12pm–5pm

JP¥

¥ ¥

W

kitone.jp

In a tranquil pocket next to Byodo-ji temple, a hinged garage door lifts up to reveal this secret store. The cult of kitone reaches way beyond Kyoto. National and international tastemakers visit for the store's small but artfully collected cache of vintage and new ceramics, homewares, handmade accessories, clothes and oddments. There's no specific theme – it's whatever captures the owner's attention – and they have a keen eye here for the best in simple quality. The store is rustic and pocket-sized, and you'll have to sidle your way around tables and cabinets, manouvering your bags and backpacks so as not to send this or that precious object flying off a shelf. The loss of the cafe, once housed in a corner of the store, will be felt by many, but there are great finds among the range of ceramics (you'll find your ultimate teapot or breakfast bowl here among the rustic pottery); the rack full of beautifully curated linen clothing; and the zakka (miscellaneous lifestyle items) – from fiercely independent and local makers – all of which will bring you to this peaceful enclave.

minä perhonen
ミナ ペルホネン

Revered Japanese designer's store over four floors in a 1920s building.

1F 251-2 Ichinomachi Shijo-sagaru
Kawaramachi-dori Shimogyo-ku

600 7737

Kyoto-Kawaramachi Station

Fri–Wed 11am–7pm

JP¥

¥¥¥

W

mina-perhonen.jp

The Kyoto branch of minä perhonen's store is a must for fans of designer Akira Minagawa's wistful clothing and accessories made from his exquisite and, at times, boldly graphic textile designs. An impressive Showa period (1926–89) building from the 1920s–30s is devoted almost entirely to minä. The first floor is the main store – the ceiling, tiled floor and butterfly-themed doors are essential viewing even if you're not in the market for minä's clothing. Climb to the 3rd floor for **Arkistot's** jewellery and homewares selection. Covet the range in the galleria showcasing heirloom pieces from the beauty of collections past, no longer for sale. The extraordinary manipulation of fabric and delicately stitched designs are a testament to why Minagawa is revered throughout Japan and beyond. The 4th floor features minä bold piece (peer through the hole in the wall to see the makers hard at work sewing and repairing), where price-friendly fabric bags and cloth-covered buttons are standout purchases.

Artisan shopping

Shijo shopping
四条での買い物

Kyoto's central shopping mecca.

Shijo-dori has a permanently festive atmosphere, with canopies, piped music, hanging banners and seasonal displays. This is the perfect place to start the day if you need a Kyoto shopping fix. Head to DIY superstore **Tokyu Hands** (branded here as Hands Kyoto) for a prime pick of their famous selection of homewares, gadgets and gizmos. Check out **Daimaru** and **Takashimaya** for top-level department store shopping, and don't miss their basement food halls, crammed with a sensory overload of delicious food with a Kyoto twist. Daimaru's hip little sister, **Fuji Daimaru**, stocks contemporary fashion for the younger set. Sweet fans should drop by **O Tabi Kyoto** for some quality matcha soft serve or wonderfully packaged Kyoto specialties, which are perfect for gifts. With their new concept store **Standard Products**, **Daiso** has moved into the homewares market, going up against the likes of **Muji** and **Ikea** with practical and affordable travel bags, camping gear, laundry tools and kitchen utensils, bathroom towels, bedroom linens and a tempting range of cute and cuddly things for your pets.

Heading towards Gion, you'll find some smaller zakka (miscellaneous lifestyle items) stores. **Handkerchief Bakery** has hot handkerchiefs, and **Karancolon Kyoto** and **RAAK** have great fabric bags and scarves made with Kyoto-designed textiles.

Artisan shopping

Karaku

日本華道社

Ikebana tools and books on the temple grounds where ikebana was created.

———————————————

8th floor, Ikenobo
Headquarters Bldg
235 Donomaecho, Rokkaku-dori
Nakagyo-ku

223 0613

Karasuma Oike

Mon–Sat 9am–6pm

JP¥
¥ ¥

W
kadosha.co.jp

One of the highest forms of mindful practice in Japan, ikebana combines the spiritual teachings of Buddhism with the careful placement of bud, branch and stem. In stark contrast to Western-style flower arranging, ikebana is a meditation on form, evoking the inner beauty and spirit of flowers to present the fragility of nature in a precious tableau. Rokka-ku temple, dating back over 1400 years, is the birthplace of ikebana and the home of the Ikenobo Society of Floral Art. You'll also find Nihon Kadosha's ikebana store, Karaku on the 8th floor of the Ikenobo Headquarters Building on the temple grounds. This no-nonsense store sells the popular ikebana shears, kenzan (pinholders for placement of flowers), tape, vases and a range of books, including the popular *Ikenobo* magazine. The ikebana enthusiast will find all of their needs catered for, and others can find the perfect gifts to take back to anyone who wants to begin developing their own floral art skills.

SOWGEN
ソウゲン

A treasure trove of repurposed vintage bric-a-brac.

573 Takamiyacho
Nakagyo-ku

252 1007

Kyoto-Kawaramachi

Mon–Sun 11.30am–7pm

JP¥

¥ ¥

W

sowgen.com

A roller door creaks open to reveal a jumbled, ramshackle curiosity shop of oddments, vintage lights and furniture. SOWGEN is like a dark, mysterious flea market (offset by the striking greens of houseplants) showcasing vintage Kyoto, and tastefully sourced to reflect up-to-the-minute styles. As you enter, you're likely to see someone mending or refurbishing a used item that will soon be re-fit for purpose – whether it's for original use or as an inspiring display piece remains to be seen. The tables, stools, display cabinets and chairs are the stars, a stroll through the last 200 years of rustic, hand-made Kyoto. The en-point furniture and bric-a-brac, tools and small household objects like hooks, clasps, picture frames, bowls, typewriters, blackboards, mirrors, toys and more will have you fossicking for hours for the pieces that will give your home some serious Kyoto-ness. The atmospheric cafe at the back reflects the rustic, atmospheric store and is a great place to relax with a drink, and ponder how you will arrange your new purchases when you get home.

Artisan shopping

Lisn
リスン

Contemporary incense store selling a bento box of scents.

COCON Kurasuma
620 Karasuma Shijo
Shimogyo-ku

353 6466

Karasuma

Mon–Sun 11am–8pm

JP¥
¥ ¥

W
lisn.co.jp

Shh. At Lisn they humbly ask you to 'listen' to the fragrances. It's an invitation to relax and let the heavenly scents speak to you. Lisn is the contemporary face of Kyoto's famous 300-year-old Shoyeido incense store, and its timeless beauty has been brought into the now with exquisite packaging and delicate new spins on traditional aromas. Scents are named to reflect the moods and memories they evoke. Amongst our favourites from the over 150 scents on offer are 'Foggy Resinoid,' and the 'Smoketone' and 'Universe' series. The store is extraordinary. Walls curve like smoke, alien lights diffuse an other-worldly glow and shelves hang in the air like a waft of incense. Buyers' pick is the bento-like box containing a selection of Lisn's most popular and most engaging scents. It's the perfect omiyage (local souvenir), and a great way to bring the sweet smells of Kyoto home with you.

Kamiji Kakimoto
紙司柿本

Longstanding paper store for the stationery obsessive.

310 Shimohakusancho
Nakagyo-ku

211 3481

Kyoto Shiyakusho-mae

Tues–Sun 9.30am–5pm

JP¥
¥¥

W
kyoto-kakimoto.jp

Japan is well known for its washi, or beautiful handmade paper. Craft capital Kyoto has spent years perfecting the art, and there's something about the quality and the tactile nature of the paper that makes it akin to a textile. Established in 1845 in the late Edo period (1603–1867), Kakimoto is a focal point for crafters, folders, writers, and lovers of all things paper. You'll see people gently feeling the sensual, textural nature of the paper between their fingers. Slide out the thin drawers and gasp at the breadth of colours, patterns, fibres and weaves. They specialise in yuzen (traditional hand-dyed paper) and kizuki-gami, which is made entirely from tree bark. All paper comes in different sizes, including popular small squares known as kaishi. Watch the staff show off their own paper-folding skills as they wrap your purchases in the Japanese diagonal wrapping style. Seasonal spins on stationery, writing pads and novelty items are very popular as take-home gifts.

Artisan shopping

Teramachi shopping

寺町会商店街

Kyoto's 'art avenue' is a vintage shopping adventure.

Often called 'Craft Street' or 'Art Avenue', Teramachi-dori is one of Kyoto's unmissable shopping opportunities. It's a street in two acts. Spill out of the eastern end of Nishiki Market (see p. 63) into South Teramachi, a covered arcade with food joints, clothing stores, cheap and cheerful souvenirs and the odd treasure. Rubber-stamp enthusiasts should head to **Tamaru Inbou**, who have been in the stamp business for more than a hundred years. The Japanese gods range is very popular (come on, you know you want that monkey flying on a cloud stamp). Don't miss picturesque **Horaido**, a longstanding tea shop where genmaicha was invented. There's a pocket in the middle of Teramachi that is vintage music heaven, and **Poco a Poco**, **Happy Jack**, **Workshop Records**, **Hard Bop**, and the uniquely named **100000t alonetoco** have outstanding collections of used vinyl, CDs and books. Built up an appetite? **Naruto Taiyaki Hompo** is a picturesque stall that sells piping hot fish-shaped waffles filled with red-bean paste or custard.

Northern Teramachi, across Nijo-dori, is the top end in every sense, lined with long-established paper, textiles, calligraphy and tea stores. Calligraphy buffs should head to **Kobaien**, where they have been making ink and brushes for more than 400 years. Store highlights include racks of hanging brushes in all sizes and impressively ornate ink slates. **Banterra** sells superlative goods made from bamboo or wood. **Kyoto Antiques Center** is a bazaar with many separate stalls selling dolls, statuettes, temple bells, kimonos, ceramics and more. For ethnic clothing and homewares, plus an assortment of small latches, doorknobs, hinges and hooks, head into **Granpie**. You'll easily fill a day exploring these streets and your suitcase will be hard to close by the time you've finished shopping here.

Artisan shopping

Zohiko Urushi Art

京漆匠 象彦

This lacquerware is the Kyoto purchase that you will treasure forever.

719–1 Yohojimaecho
Nakagyo-ku, Kyoto

229 6625

Kyoto Shiyakusho-mae

Wed–Mon 10am–6pm

JP¥

¥ ¥ ¥

W

zohiko.co.jp

Zohiko's famous maki-e lacquerware technique, dating to the 1600s, is the pinnacle of the craft. Don't let the modern façade deceive you. The minimalist elegance of the fit-out perfectly showcases their mastery of Kyoto lacquerware. It feels like you are walking through a family's history, with current proprietor Nishimura Hikobei being the 10th generation of owners. Tea ceremony wares and utensils are exquisite, as are the highly decorative boxes, plates and the elegant squares perfect for that single wagashi (Japanese sweet). The must-buy product is the sake cup (for drinking cold sake) featuring monthly motifs re-creating the seasons through emblems of nature. Themes include lingering snow for February and July's *'milky way flowing through the night sky'* – shaped and carved from a single piece of wood (and available as a set in a beautiful gift box). The insightful in-store display takes you through the process of untreated to perfect lacquerware. The store also has an eye to the future with co-labs producing unique fountain pens and watches.

Gallery Kei
GALLERY啓

Vintage textile and fabric shop with museum-quality pieces and an amiable owner.

464 Teramachi-dori
Kuoninmaecho
Nakagyo-ku

212 7114

Kyoto Shiyakusho-mae

Mon–Sat 11.30am–6pm,
Sun 12-6pm

JP¥
¥¥

W
gallerykei.jp

Passionate collector Kawasaki Kei has put together a museum-level collection of vintage textiles and fabrics. The materials and dyes, the result of centuries of perfection, are miles away from the machine-made techno-fabrics of today. Pieces are priced according to their age, rarity and intricacy, so you can pay over ¥3000 for an offcut, but every piece tells its own story, and prices aren't likely to faze textile purists in search of a piece of Kyoto history. Noren (traditional fabric curtains), matsuri (festival) happi coats and indigo-dyed fabrics hang on walls or sit in piles around the store, just waiting to be re-discovered. Ask Kei-san about the pieces as she knows the provenance of each one and she themes her materials to create in-store exhibits, so it's a history lesson just walking through the doors.

Artisan shopping

Kohchosai Kosuga
公長齋小菅

*The most exquisite
woven bamboo items
you'll ever see.*

74 Nakajimcho
Nakagyo-ku

221 8687

Sanjo

Mon–Sun 11am–5.30pm

JP¥

¥ ¥ ¥

W

kohchosai.co.jp

With a history dating back to 1898 (founder Kocho Ueda was court painter to the 11th Tokugawa feudal lord), Kohchosai's immaculate woven bamboo homewares would look more at home on museum pedestals. The fashion bags, flower baskets and tiered boxes are like delicate woven wood webs and premium artworks that draw on skills and knowledge learnt over many centuries. You'll be desperate to pick them up but scared to at the same time. Some items run at a high price point, but there are affordable items as well, especially within the delicate range of chopsticks and smoothly crafted cutlery, all of which make perfect gifts or mementos of Kyoto. The store also specialises in incense, and the ceramic incense holder with woven bamboo casing is a must buy. The chikuseiko charcoal incense is made from bamboo and has a delicious smoky forest scent – a very unique Kyoto keepsake.

Naito Brush Shop
桔梗利 内藤商店

Specialist 19th-century store selling straw and bamboo cleaning tools.

26 Nakajimacho
Nakagyo-ku

221 3018

Sanjo

Mon–Sun 9.30am–7.30pm

JP¥

¥

Step back in time to a world where houses were swept clean with hardy brushes and brooms made from straw and bamboo. Founded in 1818 (by a samurai no less), the store is now run by the seventh-generation of an old Kyoto family. Perched on the street just before spectacular and ancient Sanjo bridge, Naito Brush Shop is a small sparse room where brooms hang in bundles, brushes come in all shapes and sizes and small household cleaning tools sit in racks and boxes just as they did centuries ago. The tools instore are selected from specialist regions around Japan, or made exclusively for the store by artisans and are immaculately hand-crafted. Vegetable and dishwashing brushes (and toilet brushes) all come with a charm and elegance that might actually inspire you to clean. Tiny wooden hand-held brush and shovel sets make great gifts. The straw bundle brushes are amazing and a witch would be proud to ride one; you might purchase one to display rather than sully it with your household dirt.

Artisan shopping

Comme des Garçons
コム デ ギャルソン

An alien black cube has landed in the backstreets of Kyoto.

378 Kameyacho
Nakagyo-ku

223 0370

Kyoto Shiyakusho-mae

Mon–Sun 11am–8pm

JP¥

¥ ¥ ¥

W

comme-des-garcons.com

Set between traditional Kyoto buildings, a sci-fi, glossy black box shimmers like an oasis, materialising into Kyoto's latest Comme des Garçons store. Like a giant replica of Comme's iconic scent bottles, the Tardis-like cube becomes a portal to a minimalist plane where you'll find racks of Rei Kawakubo's high end, inventive, art school meets samurai fashion creations. Enter through a curved tunnel, and into the space that feels more like a gallery than a store; this feeling doesn't change as you peruse the exquisitely challenging designs. The walls are sparse, daubed occasionally with soft street art splatters that fall across the various counters, and on one wall you'll find contemporary black and white silk screen graffiti by American conceptual artist Adam Pendleton. Collabs and Japan-only collections are available with pop-culture riffs on The Beatles and Mickey Mouse. Macoto Takahashi's shojo-style artwork adorns an ever-popular range of skirts and T-shirts. Emerging from the black cube into the sunlight, you'll feel like you have stepped into a world that is the same and yet ... slightly different.

Lader

ラダー

Stylish home essentials you didn't know you needed.

67-38 Nishinokyo Shokujicho
Nakagyo-ku

406 5230

Nijojo-mae

Thurs–Tues 11am–6pm

JP¥

¥ ¥

W

lader.jp

Tucked away in a quiet enclave near Nijo Castle (see p. 205), this destination store (situated adjacent to Clamp Coffee, see p. 42), has shelves and shelves of clever items. Each item has been chosen for its ability to make your home life not just easier, but way cooler. You'll find bowls, scales, whisks, peelers, chopsticks and bits and bobs you didn't know you needed, like bread-knife sharpeners and candle powered aroma diffusers. The coveted Shirokiya chopping boards, made from materials like cedar, ginko, magnolia and cat willow, come in a variety of sizes and price points – every home should have one, so select the one that suits! We picked up some of those handy thingamies that clip together and seal a packet once you've opened it. You know the ones. On the way to the counter a Yamagata apple juice and some adzuki bean bamboo charcoal salt also found their way into our basket.

Artisan shopping

Maiko Antiques
舞妓骨董店

An oddball mix of Kyoto collectibles.

157 Komatucho
Higashiyama-ku

541 2626

Kiyomizu-Gojo or
Kyoto-Kawaramachi

Sat–Sun 1–6pm,
Mon–Fri hours vary

JP¥
¥

W
maiko-antiques-kyoto.
mystrikingly.com

Maiko Antiques has one of the most oddball collections of Showa period (1926–89) vintage you will ever see. Start by rifling through the stuff out the front – the evocative samurai postcards will have you rethinking your haircut, while pre-loved yukatas (summer robes) and kimonos will complete the look. Once inside, you may wish to inform your nearest and dearest that you'll be uncontactable for the next few hours. Trawl through Japanese pop culture history, where kewpie dolls, freaky masks, matchboxes, old lanterns, books, boxes, tins and toys compete for space on overstuffed shelves. The black-and-white photographs are amazing, and it's hard to believe anyone let them go. Blush at the large range of geisha porn figurines – you're sure to learn a few new positions. Elsewhere, prosthetic limbs and false teeth offer a touch of the bizarre – if you're planning to start your own creepy science museum, you'll find some prime exhibits here. Opening hours vary during the week, so check the website.

Sfera
スフェラ

Cutting-edge, upmarket design store with traditional flair.

17 Benzaiten-cho
Higashiyama-ku

532 1105

Sanjo or Gion-Shijo

Store Thurs–Tues 10am–6pm,
Bar Mon–Sat 7pm–4am

JP¥

¥ ¥ ¥

W

ricordi-sfera.com

Not far from the heart of traditional Gion you'll find Sfera, a contemporary design store that adopts the same devotion to quality handcrafted products that Kyoto is historically famous for but updates it for the now. Beautiful one-off ceramics, tea caddies, fans, porcelain and cutlery sit on the shelves like precious gallery exhibits. Choose between numerous handmade designs – the slight imperfections in each object make them unique, so pick one that suits your personality. The kitchenware here will have you mentally upgrading your own space. Downstairs, you'll find a workspace and a cafe. Say hello to super-cute French bulldog Don. He might ignore you, though – he's famous now that he's the face of DOnG, his own range of pet products. If you're in the area at night, make sure you check out **Satonaka** on the 3rd floor, a Kyoto bar where they serve drinks in Sfera's designer glassware.

Shoyeido

松栄堂

An 18th-century specialist incense store in a beautiful building.

3-334 Kiyomizu
Higashiyama-ku

532 5590

Kiyomizu Gojo

Mon–Sun 10am–5pm

JP¥

¥¥

W

shoyeido.co.jp

Shoyeido has been crafting beautiful scents since 1705. If you're shopping for some smoky, sweet, intoxicating incense sticks, waft into the old wooden townhouse on the streets of Higashiyama's beautiful Sannen-zaka, the perfect setting for this emblematic store. Inside, the shop is minimalist modern, a blank canvas against which the colours and aromas of incense can be the star. Try before you buy. Tiny sticks of 'the pure and clean scent of lavender in the moonlight', or 'the gentle breezy scent of violets in the wilderness', are on display in small vials for you to inhale and savour. Lighting up an incense stick at home will immediately transport you back to this special part of Kyoto.

Otsuka Gofukuten

大塚呉服店

Contemporary kimono prints and styles and a killer view of Hokan-ji pagoda.

88 Hoshinocho
Higashiyama-ku

533 0533

Kiyomizu-Gojo

Mon–Sun 11am–7pm

JP¥

¥¥¥

W

otsuka-gofukuten.jp

Traditional Kyoto is getting a contemporary makeover and Otsuka Gofukuten is at the forefront, evolving the classic kimono into a modern style of dress for the Kyoto-ite on the go. Head to the Higashiyama store that boasts an optimum location, in view of one of Kyoto's iconic sights – the Hokan-ji pagoda. Snap some pics and then head in to peruse Otsuka's premium collection. Their three-step price system, from casual to sophisticated, will give you room to move, and with kimonos in contemporary checks and stripes and updates on the more traditional patterns, it's a safe bet that whether you want to wear your kimono shopping or out to dinner, there will be something here for you. Why not pair your modern kimono with one of their capes? Add footwear from the range of geta (wooden sandals) in surprisingly bold colours. Accessories, including umbrellas and handbags, will complete your new look.

Artisan shopping

Kiso Artech
木曽アルテック社

*Premium handmade
wooden homewares on
the Philosopher's Path.*

43 Honenincho Shishigatani
Sakyo-ku

751 7175

Keage

Mon–Sun 9.30am–5.30pm

JP¥
¥¥

W
kiso-artech.co.jp

Kiso Artech has added its own quiet beauty
to the Philosopher's Path (see p. 19) – the
perfect place for a store that prides itself
on the most immaculate craftsmanship.
The name comes from the merging of art,
technology and the famed Japanese cyprus
from the Kiso mountains. The woodcraft is
impeccable – delicate shoehorns, impossibly
light wooden cups, handmade Edobitsu rice
holders and rough-hewn chopping boards are
all formed lovingly from 'Kiso Hinoki' and other
local timbers. The range of lacquerware and
ceramics is the epitome of a refined Japanese
aesthetic and you'll want to buy everything.
The building mirrors the quality: a modern
Japanese exterior overlooks the flowing
canal and channels the Zen atmosphere of the
Philosopher's Path. The interior reflects the
surrounding beauty of the seasons – berries
and seedpods are strewn in and about the
products, bringing the outside in.

Essence Kyoto
エッセンス キョウト

*Local makers of
tableware and homewares
in Higashiyama's
delightful north.*

2F 36-1 Okazaki Enshojicho
Sakyo-ku

744 0680

Higashiyama

Tues–Sun 11am–6pm

JP¥

¥ ¥

W

essencekyoto.com

Looking for prestigious, unique ceramics, tableware and homewares handmade by individual, local artists? Head to North Higashiyama where Essence Kyoto presides over a chic enclave, lovingly gazing out over the canal surrounding the Rohm Theatre (see p. 208) and Okazaki Park. Opened in November 2018, the store exhibits like a gallery, showing group collections and works by solo makers. The pieces are available for purchase, and the price point for these unique, superbly crafted works might surprise you. Peruse the quality work and to read interviews (in English) with the artists. Takemata's cutlery is elegantly crafted, and the Teppei Ono ceramic collection will immediately win your heart – silently hope that there are some pieces available in these popular artist's collections when you visit. Essence Kyoto also sell pesticide-free Japanese tea leaves. The tea comes in envelopes or cannisters and includes single-origin tea, premium pan-fried green tea and single-origin black tea. Essence Kyoto also has an online shop with international shipping.

Artisan shopping

Ouchi
京都おうち

Everyday-use items are elevated in this sophisticated space.

50-1 Okazaki Kitagoshocho
Sakyo-ku

751 7550

Jingu-Marutamachi

Mon–Sun 10.30am–4pm

JP¥

¥ ¥

W

instagram.com/ouchi_kyoto

Ouchi's small gallery-like space is a pilgrimage for devotees of quality homewares and designer goods and commands a quiet respect as soon as you enter. The attention to detail and sophisticated level of curation in this store pay homage to the grandeur of the nearby **Heian-jingu shrine** (see p. 158). A wood panel entrance under white or red noren (traditional fabric curtains) – depending on the season – leads to the dark and peaceful enclave of a beautiful old, repurposed machiya (traditional wooden townhouse). Slip off your shoes and drift about the store, perusing shelves of woven baskets, brushes, stockpots, saucepans, ceramics and steamers, tea towels, trivets and tempura drainers. The bamboo-ware is exquisite and all items have that Kyoto hand-made elegance. There is also a smattering of clothing, linen dresses and sustainable ware. If you are looking for a special piece, splash some yen on a teapot or rice cooker, or start your collection of small, precious kitchenware items.

Kamisoe
かみ添

Chic paper store run by a shoji screen expert.

11-1 Higashi Fujinomori-cho
Murasakino Kita-ku

432 8555

Kuramaguchi

Tues–Sun 12pm–6pm

JP¥

¥¥

W

kamisoe.com

Ko Kado runs this small, elegant paper shop in north Kyoto – he's one of the new makers that's moved into the area. He takes his knowledge of graphics and block print onto paper, which he then uses to adorn beautiful shoji screens. In an era of mass production, it's refreshing to see someone lovingly crafting traditional objects by hand and adding a contemporary twist – blending craftsmanship with modern design. But you don't have to be in need of a shoji screen to enjoy this shop. One of the great things about Kamisoe is that shoji paper is also used for stationery. The exquisite paper is repurposed into notepads and envelopes with the quality of times gone by. Pick up some stationery for unique omiyage (regional souvenir).

Artisan shopping

お土産

OMIYAGE

Omiyage (local products) is an incredibly important part of Japanese culture. Essentially souvenirs for gift giving, the ritual is so much more than just bringing back a trinket or sending a postcard. Travelling to another city or region and not returning laden with gifts for your boss, work colleagues and loved ones would be unthinkable. Most omiyage are food related, sweets in particular, but bringing back a specialty item with no expiry date that reflects the craft of the region, can earn you extra points. The box it comes in is also important. Beautifully packaged regional food, drink and craft specialities can be found at train stations and throughout each of the country's towns and cities. We like to allow an extra hour on the day we arrive at Kyoto Station on the shinkansen (bullet train) as we need to 'spend time with the omiyage'.

The choices are plentiful – sake from Fushimi, tea from Uji, packaged sweets, cakes, dried foods, geisha hair products and stage actor make-up, as well as artisan creations, textiles, wood crafting and lacquerware, are items that you can't leave Kyoto without. Remember, it's probably a good idea to buy one of everything for yourself as well …

For international travellers: we have included Kyoto local (and lightweight) speciality items, but check customs' regulations about taking food items home.

Kyoto Station
京都駅

Omiyage (regional souvenirs) became prevalent in Japan with the advent of fast trains and, as a result, some of the best places to pick up souvenirs are at train stations. Kyoto Station is no exception. Outside the gate, stores vie for your attention with an array of pretty things to scoop up before you leave Kyoto. On the 1st floor and basement floor of **The Cube** mall, as well as at **Asty Rd** arcade (inside and outside the ticket gates), you'll find souvenir stores like **Koto Miyabi**, **Kyo-No-Miyabe** and **Kyoto Shinise No-Aji-Maiko**, all selling beautifully presented boxes of yatsuhashi and ajari-mochi (rice flour triangles with a sweet bean paste centre) – an iconic Kyoto treat. Dango rice flour dumplings, senbei crackers and tsukemono (pickles) come in a variety of sizes, shapes and flavours. Kyoto's famous Kyo-yaki pottery is also available, along with tenegui/furoshiki (cloth wrapping), paper fans and incense. **Isetan** food hall also showcases plenty of Kyoto-only must-buys.

Inside the shinkansen (bullet train) gates, gift stores line the corridors. You'll find specialty sake from Fushimi, green tea products from Uji (see p. 217), kawaii (cute) socks, bags and accessories using traditional Japanese fabrics, lacquerware, woodcraft and sake vessels, along with various other Kyoto-themed curiosities. A Kyoto Tower keyring, perhaps? The gold box of the **Malebranche** (see p. 147) shop in ASTY allows you to pick up delectable last-minute green tea sweets, superbly wrapped for maximum effect. And if you're running out of luggage space, outside Kyoto Station you'll find a large **Japan Post Office**, if you feel the need to send packages home.

Higashishiokoji
Kamadonocho
Shimogyo-ku

Kyoto

General: 8am–8pm
Counters: 5.30am–
11.30pm

JP¥
¥ ¥

W
Jr-odekake.net

Omiyage

Seien Daigokudenhompo

大極殿本舗 六角店 栖園

Longstanding sweet store with seasonal noren curtains whose colours reflect the flavours of the sweets.

Opening in 1885, Daigokuden is where Kyoto locals go to buy elegant sweets for special occasions. The exterior is an unmissable Rokkaku-dori landmark. The subtle tones of the mushiko (insect cage) wooden slat window that spans the entire frontage are beautifully offset by brightly coloured noren (traditional fabric curtains). Inside, antique cabinets are filled with tiny delights, including an extensive range of higashi (sweet cakes) made into vibrant seasonal and symbolic shapes in kashigata (traditional sweet molds), the most exquisite omiyage. The noren outside change with the seasons, announcing the fruit syrup that flavours the popular shaved ice or agar jelly which can be enjoyed in the cafe with the perfect blend of tea. We've had amazake syrup in March, plum liquor in June, chestnut in October and persimmon in November. Sencha and matcha are also served with zenzai – warm red bean soup with mochi (sweet rice cakes) floating in it.

On a trip with friends, Michelle was disappointed to find the store closed. The owner was sweeping outside, and seeing Michelle's disappointment, went inside and brought out some sweets for them to try. You won't forget the Daigokuden experience.

120 Horinoecho
Rokkaku-dori
Nakagyo-ku

221 3311

Karasuma Oike

Thurs–Tues 9.30am–6pm

JP¥
¥ ¥

W
instagram.com/
daigokuden.seien

Omiyage

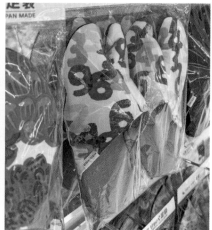

Sou Sou
ソウソウ

Kyoto fashion empire selling graphic kimonos, famous tabi socks and boots.

583-3 Nakanocho
Nakagyo-ku

212 8805

Kyoto-Kawaramachi

Mon–Sun 11am–8pm

JP¥
¥ ¥

W
sousou.co.jp

Renowned Kyoto textile design house, Sou Sou creates its own vibrant and colourful patterns to adorn clothing based on classic kimono, yukata (summer cotton kimono) and monks' working clothes, plus designs for the new – smart phone covers, purses, notebooks and more. Perfect for gifts, people flock to the store to grab their famous tabi (split toe socks) that come in a range of vivid patterns. Footwear here is also an eye-opener. Check out the geta boots, a hybrid Japanese toe sandal, crossed with trainers or gumboots and completed with Sou Sou's vibrant colours and designs. The main storefront is instantly recognisable: a yellow square covered in a spray of jumbled black numbers – the famous Sou Sou logo which you can find on many of their creations. This area just off the main streets has been dubbed Sou Sou St by the locals – you'll find seven diverse stores in this cute little enclave which allows you to explore the complete Sou Sou range.

Nijiyura
にじゆら

Contemporary Japanese specialist fabric store.

---

38 Benkeiishicho
Nakagyo-ku

253 0606

Kyoto Shiyakusho-mae

Tues–Sun 1am–6pm

JP¥
¥

W
nijiyura.com

Tenugui are long, rectangular fabric pieces traditionally used for washcloths, dishcloths or even headbands (especially in Kendo, where they function as sweatbands). These days, tenugui has become the perfect eco-wrapping for souvenirs, gifts or bottles of sake or beer. Nijiyura combines traditional dyeing and pattern-making techniques with contemporary materials, so you get the best of both worlds! This adorable little store just off Sanjo-dori has a range of patterns, from colourful abstracted animals, birds and nature to more traditional Japanese emblems perfect for omiyage (and gifts for that special someone or yourself). In-store displays will show you how to manipulate your cloth into a carry bag, lunch box or wine holder. We like to use them as wall hangings or for environmentally kind wrapping for gifts for friends – the tenugui becomes an important part of the gift itself.

Ippodo
一保堂茶舗

One of the oldest and most-respected tea shops in Japan.

---

52 Tokiwagi-cho
Nakagyo-ku

211 4018

Kyoto Shiyakusho-mae

Mon–Fri 10am–5pm

JP¥
¥ ¥

W
ippodo-tea.co.jp

Three centuries of selling tea 'blessed by mother nature' and picked in the fertile local tea fields has made Ippodo one of the most respected and memorable tea sellers in Japan. The elegant dark wooden exterior with Ippodo's Kanji namesake splashed over noren (traditional fabric curtains) is iconic, as are the staff's immaculate uniforms and flawless service. If you're in Kyoto at Christmastime, queue for their limited-edition New Year tea – a Kyoto custom and the perfect Kyoto omiyage! Ippodo sells teapots, whisks, cups and canisters, all perfect to take home as gifts or keepsakes. Tea varieties at Ippodo are extensive (sencha, matcha, hojicha, genmaicha and more), and you can experience them in the cafe, where tea comes in a set with a seasonal sweet (our favourite is geranium). If you choose a sencha or bancha, it will arrive with a small teapot, three teacups and a timer. Phrases like 'tea leaves unravelling', 'do not agitate' and 'the last drop is best' are whispered with reverence. If you're curious about which teas are cultivated in the shade or open field, book in for a tea class or tasting session.

Kyukyodo

鳩居堂

Specialist incense and stationery stores perfect for buying gifts.

520 Shimohonnojimaecho
Nakagyo-ku

231 0510

Kyoto Shiyakusho-mae

Mon–Sun 10am–6pm

JP¥

¥ ¥

W

kyokyodo.co.jp

Dating back over 350 years, with origins as a pharmacy that evolved into a stationer for the Imperial Palace, Kyukyodo's creative history is reflected in its premium range of stationery, incense and washi paper. A Kyoto stalwart, it has undergone a striking reboot with two stores straddling the covered arcade of Teramachi-dori. Beautiful light and dark wood frontages reveal interiors with soaring wood-slat ceilings and diffused, atmospheric lighting. To your left as you head north is the store that specialises in incense. Deep smoky aromas caress you as you enter and the room is warmed by traditional-style lamp lighting. Weave your way in and around the shelves, where you'll find incense in many forms, as well as calligraphy tools, paper and cards. Have your own hanko (name) stamp made or pick up some notebooks, bamboo or lacquerware calligraphy brushes or geisha bookmarks. Across the way, you'll find the stationery specialist store selling various types of paper, cards and washi tape, as well as bags and general store merchandise.

Uchu Wagashi Teramachi
ウチュウ ワガシ 寺町本店

A modern store selling bold,
brightly coloured sweets.

307 Shintomicho
Kamigyo-ku

754 8538

Jingu-Marutamachi

Thurs–Mon 10am–5pm

JP¥

¥

W

uchu-wagashi.jp

If Mondrian or Matisse had made candy it would look something like Uchu Wagashi's boxed creations. Bold, bright and graphic, the candy makes a surprising and unique Kyoto take-home gift. Their speciality is wasanbon and konpeito, hard candy made from sugar and rice flour that melts slowly in your mouth. Shapes echo Japan's graphic past and many notable symbols and everyday objects are given a contemporary makeover. Box sets come at affordable price points and include adorable tiny fish, birds, aeroplanes, houses, flowers and even hot-air balloons. The 'drawing candy' is great fun: vividly coloured puzzle pieces that can be rearranged into objects and animals. This shop, Uchu's main store on north Teramachi-dori, mirrors the tiny Uchu candy boxes. Arrange yourself into the warm, wooden cube-like structure. There is a small area where you can sit and enjoy a colourful pop-themed soda, looking at a beautiful small-scale Japanese garden, while considering which of your friends deserves one of their sweet, pop-colour candy sets.

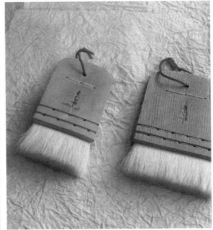

Yojiya
よーじや

Historic make-up store loved by actors and geisha.

270 Gionmachi
Higashiyama-ku

541 0177

Gion-Shijo

Mon–Thurs 10.30am–6.30pm,
Fri–Sun 10.30am–7pm

JP¥

¥ ¥

W

yojiya.co.jp

Since 1904, Kyoto's Yojiya has provided stage make-up for performers and film actors, and over the years their iconic black and white face in a mirror logo has become one of Kyoto's most recognisable symbols. While perusing the shelves of luxury make-up in-store you might find yourself shopping next to a plain-clothes geisha, a famous stage actor or the beauty-obsessed elite, so it's a good place to people watch as well as pick up a precious Kyoto souvenir. The go-to omiyage purchase is the blotting paper, available in small, portable packs, invented to help stage actors maintain skin cleanliness by removing harmful oils and keeping their make-up from running while performing (also comes in handy for travellers, especially during summer). You can also buy soap, handcream, lip gloss and make-up accessories, all in Yojiya's tasteful packaging. We love going to the cafe, where the logo emblazons parfait and cappuccinos, and delightful sandwich squares come in a jubako lacquer box, all unmissable photo opportunities.

Omiyage

Kazurasei
かづら清

Making hair products and combs for geisha for over a century.

---

285 Gionmachi north
Shijo-dori
Higashiyama-ku

561 0672

Gion-Shijo

Mon–Tues & Thurs–Sun
10am–6pm

JP¥

¥ ¥

W

kazurasei.co.jp

While the mysteries of Kyoto's geisha may be impenetrable, you can learn one or two secrets when you shop at Kazurasei. Yin to Yojiya's (see p. 145) yang, Kazurasei keeps a low profile, exuding a discreet air of luxury and tradition. This shop is old-school Gion, and has been serving the local geisha since 1865, making sure the trademark complex geisha hair is immaculate. Kazurasei stocks hair accessories – check out the boxwood combs and ornamental lacquer hairpins, some which belong in a museum, and are priced accordingly. The omiyage holy grail here is the magical hair balm, tsubaki oil, made from the prized camellia nut. This elixir has kept geisha hair beautiful for hundreds of years and it is well worth investing in a bottle or two. Locals swear by this top beauty secret. The camellia nut oil also features in shampoos and skincare products. If you're prone to dry lips, pick up some of their honey and safflower lip balm.

Malebranche Kitayama Main Store
マールブランシュ京都北山本店

Kyoto's favourite delicately packaged matcha biscuits.

40 Iwagakakiuchicho
Kamigamo
Kita-ku

722 3399

Matsugasaki

Mon–Sun 9am–6pm

JP¥

¥

W

malebranche.co.jp

Opening as a cafe in 1951, Malebranche quickly became the go-to spot for French-inspired sweets with a Japanese twist. The Kitayama main store, in Kyoto's north, opened in 1982, a sleek, modern enclave where you can eat in, or takeaway lemon tarts or madelines and, if they haven't sold out, their hugely popular Mont Blanc. Proudly perched at the front of the Botanical Gardens (see p. 176), Malebranche is perfect for picking up picnic delights. Their cha-no-ka, a green tea flavoured langue de chat (French-style biscuit) with a soft white chocolate centre, has evolved into one of the most requested Kyoto omiyage. An east-meets-west, traditional-meets-modern sliver of delight, it has an irresistible, delicate flavour. Buy a box for friends (and it goes without saying, one for yourself). Note: there is also a small Malebranche outlet in **ASTY** inside Kyoto Station (see p. 137) where you can buy last-minute cha-no-ka in beautifully wrapped gift boxes before you leave Kyoto.

早起きの人へ

FOR EARLY RISERS

Kyoto is a mellow-paced city that likes to gently rise at a respectable hour, so early morning breakfast and activities can be a little hard to come across for travellers who wake with the sun (or are jet-lagged). That being said, there is a plethora of memorable experiences waiting for those in the know. Bells call monks to prayer on temple grounds, like at sprawling Higashi Hongan-ji (see p. 153) and Kyomizu-dera (see p. 157). Forest pathways normally awash with daytrippers, such as the mega-popular Sagano Bamboo Grove in Arashiyama (see p. 160), are nearly empty, a special tranquillity settling over them in the breaking morning.

If you need that early wake-me-up caffeine fix, great seats can be found at kissaten (retro coffee houses), like Inoda Coffee Honten (see p. 155) and Coffee House Maki (see p. 159), and contemporary cafes and coffee spots like Weekenders Coffee Tominokoji (see p. 156)and Lower East 9 Cafe (see p. 152), where you'll have a wonderful chance to share space with local Kyoto going about its morning business, stretching and rubbing its collective eyes before launching headlong into the day.

Lower East 9 Cafe

ザ ロウワー イースト ナイン カフェ

An ultra-cool New York–style hostel south of Kyoto Station with a sideline in excellent coffee.

32 Higashikujo
Minamikarasuma-cho
Minami-ku

644 9990

Kujo

Mon–Sun 8am–11pm

JP¥

¥

W

lowereastnine.com

Happily dwelling on the corner of a vast intersection a stone's throw from Kujo station, Lower East 9 is the poster hostel and cafe for the reinvented Kyoto Station south. A cosy cafe serves the public as well as the hostel's lodgers. The sparse, minimalist space is warmed up with vintage furniture, comfy couches and the welcoming smiles of the friendly staff. LE9's excellent coffee starts brewing at 8am, making it the perfect morning coffee haunt south side. At night, the happy hour is fuelled by well-priced booze and complemented by a soundtrack of the latest smooth grooves. In the afternoon or evening, find a window seat and sink into one of the cosy green velvet chairs, order a craft beer while reading the latest Kyoto lifestyle mag, or order a glass of wine and mingle with a relaxed, cool crowd of locals and international travellers.

Higashi Hongan-ji temple
東本願寺

Sprawling temple complex with the world's largest wooden roof.

754 Tokiwa-machi
Shimogyo-ku

371 9181

Kyoto

Mon–Sun 6.20am–4.30pm

JP¥
¥

W
higashihonganji.or.jp

Headquarters for one of the most popular sects of Buddhism in Japan, Jodo-shin (True Pure Land), Higashi Hongan-ji's black iron gates, beckon you into this unmissable temple compound. The major drawcard, the spectacular main hall, built in 1591, is the largest wooden structure in Kyoto and props up the largest wooden roof in the world. The massive open space features impressively thick wooden beams with ornate headpieces lit by gigantic hanging lanterns. Splendid Nishi Hongan-ji to the west boasts the impressive Goeido Hall and Amidado Hall and a secret gem: the floating cloud pavilion, dating back to the early Edo period (1603–1867). Nearby is a splendid centuries-old gingko tree. A block to the east you'll find Shosei-en, which is a small and peaceful 'pond stroll' garden, and an extended part of the Hongan-ji complex. It was created in 675 CE and is a good spot for some cherry blossom viewing, sans crowds.

For early risers

To-ji temple & flea market
東寺 弘法市

Southern temple with a jaw-dropping five-tiered pagoda and monthly flea market.

1 Kujocho
Minami-ku

691 3325

Toji

Mon–Sun 8am–5pm

JP¥
¥

W
toji.or.jp

Opening at 8am, To-ji temple, or 'east temple', stands on one side of the site of the Rashomon gate, the entrance to Japan's original capital. The 'west temple', Sai-ji burnt down in 1233 but To-ji remains – a testament to the striking scene that would once have greeted traders to the city with carts full of silks and spices. Dating back to 796 CE, its treasures include a breathtaking five-storey pagoda (this incarnation was built in 1644) – the tallest wooden tower in Japan – the Kondo (golden hall), with its ancient statue of Yakushi (the medicine Buddha), and the Miedo Hall. On the 21st of each month, a colourful flea market bursts into life on the usually peaceful grounds. Running from 5am (great for early risers!) until 5pm (but some stalls don't set up until 8am or 9am), you can rummage through brightly bannered stalls for vintage kimonos, '60s and '70s toys, lacquerware, fabrics, kewpie dolls, pottery, fans, swords, tea kettles and woodblock prints. A smaller antique market affectionately known as the 'junk' market, is held on the first Sunday of each month. Trust us, the treasures on offer are anything but junk.

Inoda Coffee Honten
イノダコーヒ 本店

An old-school Kyoto coffee institution, which is why the new-school kids love it.

---

140 Doyucho, Sakaimachi-dori Sanjo, Nakagyo-ku

241 0915

Karasuma Oike

Mon–Sun 7am–8pm

JP¥

¥¥

W

inoda-coffee.co.jp

An early morning breakfast is a tricky business in Kyoto, so it's a good thing iconic kissaten (retro coffee house), Inoda Coffee Honten, has you covered. Established in 1970 (Inoda Coffee dates to 1940), we can't decide if this Kyoto stalwart is old-world charm or retro time warp – probably a bit of both. Look for the iconic red coffee pot logo and the blue-and-white frontage with the huge vintage coffee grinder; it's a great photo opportunity – depending on how many bicycles are stacked out the front. Inside, waiters and waitresses are sharply dressed in immaculate uniforms, and the brown brick, dark wood and checked tablecloths will make you feel like you're at a chalet in the Alps. Join the morning crowds of girlfriends, savvy locals and long-time customers, and order cotton-filtered coffee and Inoda's famous tamago (egg) sandwiches. The excellent coffee types range from Columbian to café au lait and a classic Viennese served in tall glasses. Step back in time for your daily fix. Don't forget to buy some beans and classic logo mugs.

For early risers

Weekenders Coffee Tominokoji
ウィークエンダーズコーヒー 富小路

Perfect pitstop for an
artisan coffee brew.

560 Honeyanocho
Nakagyo-ku

746 2206

Karasuma or Kyoto-
Kawaramachi

Thurs–Tues 7.30am–6pm

JP¥

¥

W

weekenderscoffee.com

An 'off street' treasure box not far from Nishiki Market (see p. 63), Weekenders Coffee Tominokoji has inventively carved out a niche in a machiya (traditional wooden townhouse) at the back of a small carpark. Founded by Masahiro and Ayumi Kaneko in 2005, it was one of the early adopters in Kyoto's contemporary coffee space and has been wildly popular since its inception. The diminutive townhouse with its low, warm wood ceiling and cosy interior is a laboratory of sorts, brewing up drip filter, single-origin coffee that offers non-dairy options. Rest your espresso or latte on an ancient stone slab that serves as a table (Ah, Kyoto!). Pick up some geisha coffee drip bags and opera blend omiyage (regional souvenirs) on the way out. Make sure to pop into their roastery on Matsubara-dori, which takes the name to its logical conclusion and is only open on weekends, and sells freshly roasted beans.

Kyomizu-dera temple
清水寺

Iconic temple with a viewing platform set high on thick wooden beams.

1 294 Kiyomizu
Higashiyama-ku

551 1234

Kiyomizu-Gojo

Mon–Sun 6am–6pm
(6.30pm in summer, 9.30pm
for special events)

JP¥
¥

W
kiyomizudera.or.jp/en

Sitting proudly midway up the slopes of Mount Otowa, Kyomizu-dera is a blockbuster temple on many tourists to-do lists – and for good reason. The crowds gather daily to look in awe from the viewing platform that peers proudly over the treetops, or to snap shots of the astounding temple from the mountain path. It gets busy, but with a 6am opening time, you can rise early and stroll the complex in a quiet and reflective way. Kyomizu-dera is a Buddhist complex, established in 778 CE, devoted to Kannon, the goddess of mercy. The dark wooden main hall, teetering high on 168 wooden pillars among the towering trees, is one of the most spectacular sights in the world (builder's note, the floor is made from 410 cypress boards and locked together without using any nails). Don't miss Koyasunoto Pagoda, an ornate three-tiered pagoda with a dragon that protects it from fire. Its colours haven't faded since the 1633 reconstruction, so the dragon is doing its job!

For early risers

Heian-jingu shrine
平安神宮

Temple with a pond garden, the stepping stones featured in Lost in Translation *and rare turtles.*

Okazaki Nishitennocho
Sakyo-ku

761 0221

Higashiyama

Mon–Sun 6am–5pm

JP¥
¥

W
heianjingu.or.jp

A popular Meiji period (1868–1912) Shinto shrine, Heian-jingu was built in 1895 to celebrate Kyoto's 1100th birthday. For jet-lagged travellers, families with small people or early risers, you can walk through the massive red torii gate towards the shrine's open courtyard, where you'll find the entry to a wonderful pond garden which is open from 6am. Spend a melancholy and reflective morning stepping lithely across the pond on artfully arranged stepping stones, the breakout stars of Scarlett Johansson's reflective scene in *Lost in Translation*. The covered bridge across the lake is a great place to sit and contemplate the beauty of nature. Look for the rare golden soft-shell turtles that live here. There's also talk of an albino turtle, and a turtle with a coat of algae that looks like a straw raincoat – spot it and your luck will be on the rise. Like Narcissus, you can gaze at your image in the shimmering waterways, or watch the koi flitter about. In the south garden alone, there are more than 200 kinds of plants, but cherry blossom season reigns supreme here.

Coffee House Maki
コーヒーハウス マキ

A classic coffee house trades on decades of atmosphere and charm.

211 Seiryucho
Kamigyo-ku

222 2460

Demachiyanagi

Wed—Mon 8.30am—5pm

JP¥
¥

W
coffeehousemaki.jp

This is not the place for an almond skinny latte. Coffee House Maki features lovingly brewed drip-coffee made by experts and it's perfect to shake the early morning cobwebs from your head. The exterior is unmissable – a piece of real retro charm in Kyoto's north. Inside you'll find vinyl couches and warm woods accented by a grandfather clock, mock classical paintings on the walls, and vases and vintage coffee grinders on the shelves. It's cosy, so slide into a booth and listen to locals immersed in intellectual discussions and the happy chatter of the busy staff, and smell the wafting aroma of freshly brewed coffee and toasting bread. The real drawcard at Coffee House Maki is the morning set. The coffee comes with big toast, one slice hollowed out and filled with salad, egg, potato salad and a slice of ham, all which can practically be bought for loose change – perfect if you're travelling on a budget.

For early risers

Sagano Bamboo Grove
嵯峨野 竹林の小径

Iconic bamboo forest walk.

Arashiyama, Ukyo-ku

343 0548

Torroko Arashiyama

Mon–Sun 24 hours

Arashiyama's world famous 500m-long grove is a natural cluster of moso (turtle shell) bamboo lining curved pathways with reed fences and stone walls. It's one of Kyoto's busiest tourist spots, making it tricky for curious travellers who like to wander quietly. It's open 24 hours, however, making it perfect for early risers who get to bear witness to the light filtering gently through the trees and experience the silence of the holy sanctuary, broken now and then by the chirrup of a fossicking birds. The towering green bamboo spires bend and meet at the top, forming cathedral-like arches. There are endless photo opportunities here, but they won't do justice to the deep smell of wood and dirt, and the wonderful stillness. As a mini early itinerary, why not explore **Tenryu-ji temple** (see p. 163 and 173), then head through the north entrance to emerge into the bamboo grove for a morning stroll? Finish with a coffee at nearby **Arabica** which opens at 9am.

Kitano Tenmangu shrine
北野天満宮

Northern shrine with plum blossoms and a monthly market.

Bakurocho
Kamigyo-ku

461 0005

Kitano Tenmangu-mae

Tues–Sun 7am–5pm, flea market 6am–9pm (25th of every month)

JP¥

¥

W

kitanotenmangu.or.jp

Opening at 7am, Kitano Tenmangu's northern shrine makes for a great early morning escape from the tourist crowds and is a fantastic temple to explore. A looming torii gate beckons you into the resting place of Sugawara no Michizane, the first person ever to be enshrined as a god. (He's the god of academics, so say a little prayer and maybe you'll leave just that little bit smarter.) Kitano Tenmangu, built in 1607, is one of Kyoto's best viewing spots for the ume (plum) blossom, the cherry blossoms oft-overlooked cousin. If you're travelling in February, the Bai-en garden is in full flower. On 25 February geisha and maiko (apprentice geisha) come here to serve matcha and sweets and perform a tea ceremony amid the flowering plum blossoms. Also known for its maple leaves, Kitano Tenmangu's maple garden, Momiji-en, is awash with red in autumn. Treasure hunters note: Kitano Tenmangu hosts a fantastic flea market on the 25th of every month, with antiques, vintage textiles, souvenirs and great street food – and you can get there early to bag some treasures (from 6am)!

For early risers

Spiritual Kyoto
スピリチュアルな京都

Many of Kyoto's Zen temples offer some moving and memorable opportunities for the spiritually inclined traveller to partake in morning prayers, meditation, sutra copying and goshuin (temple seal collecting). Check websites before visiting for details and note that, often, a reservation is required. Zen Buddhism's central practice of zazen meditation is available at **Nanzen-ji temple** (see p. 172, every second and fourth Sunday 6–7am); at **Kennin-ji temple** (see p. 187, every second Sunday 7.30–8.30am); and at **Tofuku-ji temple** (see p. 169, every Sunday from 6am). **Enko-ji temple** (see p. 175) has zazen (meditation), plus a sermon and breakfast (for around ¥10) every Sunday – reserve the day before. Throughout the day you can watch the monks in meditation and performing the Amida chant in the main hall of **Chion-in temple** (see p. 193). Arrive at 8am at **Ryoan-ji temple** (see p. 29) to meditate upon the famous garden without the crowds and stop for tea at the nearby **Camellia Tea Ceremony Garden**. **Tenryu-ji temple** offers meditation (see p. 173, on the second Sunday of every month 9–10am). **Shunko-in** in **Myoshin-ji temple** has meditation at 10am. Buy a goshuincho (book for collecting temple seals) from the counter of most temples and then take it with you on temple visits to collect inscriptions and stamps. Your goshuincho book will be a beautiful keepsake to take home. **Rokkaku-do temple** opens at 6am and inscriptions and stamps are available in the shop; you can simply watch other people if you aren't collecting – it's fascinating.

Shinto Shrines (with red torii gates) such as **Fushimi Inari shrine** are open 24 hours. Fushimi Inari is one of Kyoto's most popular destinations; however, between 5am and 7am you will find the ancient, woodsy beauty around the torii gate tunnel especially sublime.

庭園と寺院

TEMPLES & GARDENS

A famous Japanese proverb says, 'in Zen we don't find the answers, we lose the questions', and strolling your way around Kyoto's estimated 2000 temples and shrines you'll quickly find yourself no longer searching, but instead discovering, experiencing, feeling and absorbing. You'll see why 16 of the city's temples and shrines are named by UNESCO as World Heritage Cultural Sites. Temples will be among the most impressive sights you will see in Kyoto, and feature some iconic moments, from Nanzen-ji (see p. 172) and Tofuku-ji's (see p. 169) looming wooden gates to Kinkaku-ji's temple (see p. 178) completely covered in gold plate.

Many temples also have lush, inventive gardens built by monks, emperors and samurai and some of the most sublime gardens in Kyoto reside on temple grounds. From Genko-an's circular window (see p. 177) to Enko-ji's autumn leaf viewing room (see p. 175), Kyoto's temples will instil within you the connection between nature and spirituality. Or why not pack a picnic and head to Kyoto's oft-missed northern Botanical Gardens (see p. 176). Or stroll through a Kyoto secret in plain view, Shosei-en garden (see p. 168). Turn your tech off and, as they also say in Zen, 'be a witness to your own thoughts.'

Shosei-en garden
渉成園

Rambling fairytale-like paths, teahouses and bridges make this the perfect strolling garden.

Higashitamamizucho
Shimogyo-ku

371 9210

Shichijo

Mon–Sun 9am–5pm

JP¥
¥

W
higashihonganji.or.jp

Shosei-en garden hides in plain sight. It's easy to walk past this high-walled enclave, cleverly concealed among the broad streets near Kyoto Station, as it gives the impression of being a private residence. Established in 1641, it's an addendum to the sprawling Higashi Hongan-ji complex, initially used as a meditation and relaxation retreat for the head priest, and you can see why. Part landscape garden and part Zen garden, this modestly sized space packs in some impressive sights. Two bridges (including Kaitaro, an ornate bridge covered by a beautiful cypress bark canopy) overlook Ingetsu-chi (moon crest), an expansive pond with picturesque islands where the water is broken by the spirited swishing of koi carp. A wide range of bird varieties have chosen this garden as their go-to, eco complementing the beehives that buzz with activity near Bokaka-ku (pavilion beside flowers). This ceremonial gate, constructed according to the ideals of a chashitsu (teahouse), is placed near cherry blossoms, which are vibrant in spring. An alluring view sums up Kyoto's contrasting nature – rising above the towering greenery you can see the modernist structure of Kyoto Tower.

Tofuku-ji temple
東福寺

*Southern temple revered
for its ancient gate, autumn
colours and Zen garden.*

15-778 Honmachi
Higashiyama-ku

561 0087

Tofukuji

Mon–Sun 9am–3.30pm

JP¥

¥

W

tofukuji.jp

Tofuku-ji (1236 CE) is the head temple
complex for the Rinzai sect of Buddhism.
Walking into Tofuku-ji is a memorable
moment – the Sanmon gate dates to 1425 CE,
the oldest in the world, and several of the
buildings, including a large communal lavatory,
also date to the 13th century. Tofuku-ji is a
popular autumn spot, exhibiting the vivid reds,
yellows and burnished golds of the changing
maples, which are particularly breathtaking
when viewed from the Gaunkyo or Tsutenkyo
bridges. The Zen garden, normally a solo
garden, is a four-act masterwork that
encompasses the main hall. Famed gardener
Mirei Shigemori designed the gardens in
1939, drawing on his education in Nihonga
painting, ikebana (the art of flower arranging),
the tea ceremony and incorporating Western
elements. Our favourite, the north garden,
features a checkerboard of perfectly placed
squares which punctuate a fluffy carpet of
grass, edged with domed hedges. It feels like
it could have been designed yesterday, today
or tomorrow.

Temples & gardens

Eikan-do (Zenrin-ji) temple

永観堂（禅林寺）

Tranquil temple grounds with impressive autumn colours.

Located between Nanzen-ji (see p. 172) and the entrance to the Philosopher's Path (see p. 19), Eikando is the perfect addition to your North Higashiyama itinerary. Once a villa, it was gifted to a priest in 853 CE and began a remarkable spiritual life. As the head temple of the Jōdo-shū Buddhist sect it impresses at any time, but during autumn, blazing red and yellow maples turn the grounds into a luminous, painterly canvas (check the times for the evening illuminations). The grounds will take you on many adventures, including along coloured walkways that overlook tranquil gardens and lead to grand halls with golden shrines. Look for the covered wooden stairway that houses a twisting, disappearing spiral staircase. The materiality is immaculate: wood, stone, cloth and tiles blend in perfect harmony. Trek to Taho-to pagoda, which is perched high above the temple and peaks invitingly through the trees as you ascend, rewarding your climb with impressive views of temple rooftops and out over the expanse of Kyoto. Anyone exploring Japan for Buddhist art treasures, note that Eikando has some of the best, including a mysterious Amida Buddha statue whose head turns to the side – a rare pose. Make sure you reserve time for a bowl of matcha paired with warabimochi (a type of Japanese sweet) in the teahouse on the temple grounds.

48 Eikandocho
Sakyo-ku

761 0007

Keage

Mon–Sun 9am–4pm

JP¥

¥¥

W

eikando.or.jp

Temples & gardens

Nanzen-ji temple
南禅寺

Peaceful Zen temple compound with an impressive wooden gate and a curious aqueduct.

Nanzenji Fukuchicho
Sakyo-ku

771 0365

Keage

Mon–Sun 8.40am–4pm

JP¥
¥ ¥

W
nanzenji.or.jp

The head temple of the Rinzai sect, dating back to the mid-13th century, Nanzen-ji is a living tapestry – witness to a turbulent history of war, invasion and fire. However, these days the whole area surrounding Nanzen-ji seems to radiate an intense spiritual calm. The light here is dappled and diffused through giant, whispering trees and it illuminates patches of the greenest moss. We love to walk through the impressive Sanmon gate (1628 CE) whose thick, dark wooden pillars frame the hondo (main hall). Pose for pics in the arches of the strange Meiji-period (1868–1912) aqueduct (built to ferry goods from Kyoto to Lake Biwa). The northern dry garden of the Hojo hall is attributed to Kobori Enshu, one of Japan's best-known Zen garden masters. The rocks here are said to mimic tigers crossing the water. Dusk at Nanzen-ji, when the monastery bells start to toll, is an unforgettable experience.

Hogon-in temple

宝厳院

Hidden temple with a garden revered by locals.

3-6 Sagatenryuji
Susukinobabacho
Ukyo-ku

861 0091

Arashiyama

Mon–Sun 9am–5pm

JP¥

¥ ¥

W

hogon-in.jp

A sub-temple of the sprawling Tenryu-ji complex (it is in the south-west corner of the temple grounds), Hogon-in has a well-deserved reputation as having one of the most interesting gardens in Kyoto. It was mapped out by 16th-century Zen monk Sakugen Shūryō, who shaped the garden as a perfect example of 'borrowed scenery.' Created in the popular strolling pond garden style, it abstractly mirrors many features of Arashiyama's surrounding natural wonders. Known as Shishiku No Niwa, or Lion's Roar Garden, the foliage is a crisp green in spring and summer, and shines in autumn with red and yellow maple leaves. Emerald moss adorns rocks and tree trunks and the prominent Lion Rock, which imposes itself upon the garden path. Among other delights you'll find the Sea of Suffering (a strewn pebble garden echoing human adversity), and the Animal Stones (not a rock group, but a group of rocks representing animals swimming towards Buddha). Hogon-in is perfect for an afternoon stroll, after lunch at nearby **Bread, Espresso & Arashiyama Garden** (see p. 44).

Enko-ji temple
圓光寺

*Off-the-tourist-trail autumn temple with
a tatami viewing room and bamboo forest.*

Founded in 1601 by famed shogun Tokugawa Ieyasu, Enko-ji is a Rizai sect
temple whose opening ceremony heralded the very birth of the Edo period
(1603–1868). Too northern to be on the regular tourist route, the temple
makes for a wonderful pilgrimage in any season, but especially in autumn.

As you approach the main gate, you'll find yourself in a fascinating
karesansui – a Zen dry or rock garden that symbolises a flying dragon. Inside
the garden there is a compact bamboo grove, and if you continue up the steep
hill, you will be rewarded with a stunning view that takes in Kyoto's impressive
sprawl above the top of the temple roof. You can appreciate – and contemplate –
some of Kyoto's best autumn moments in either of the tatami mat rooms to
the right and left of the garden; both feature rectangular windows that gaze
directly out onto a vibrant tableau of autumn reds and golds. If you are hunting
out suikinkutsu, underground water pots which allow you to listen in on tinkling,
musical water drops, then you will find one of Kyoto's best-known ones at Enko-ji.

📍	🚃	JP¥
13 Ichijoji Kotanicho	Ichijoji	¥ ¥
Sakyo-ku		
	🕐	W
📞	Mon–Sun 9am–5pm	enkouji.jp/en
781 8025		

Temples & gardens

Botanical Gardens
京都府立植物園

Northern plant lovers'
paradise with a
toadstool library.

Shimogamo Hangicho
Sakyo-ku

701 0141

Kitayama

Mon–Sun 9am–5pm

JP¥
¥ ¥

On a fine day, grab a picnic basket, stuff it
with sushi and sake, and head to the Botanical
Gardens. It's a great escape – and people
seem to have forgotten it exists, so you could
be wandering alone through the iris garden,
bonsai exhibits, lotuses, peonies, roses and
various exotics. Spend time hunting through
the incredible list of represented species. It's
fascinating to contrast the more Western,
contemporary style of garden with the many
ancient Japanese gardens. The low entry fee
is worth it for the huge conservatory alone.
The children's play area is a special treat too:
it has tall, colourful toadstools, which open
up, revealing libraries of vintage children's
books. Photograph loved ones peeking out
from behind the giant, magical fungi! The
gardens are also a good spot for sakura
(cherry blossom) viewing, notable because
the blossoms hold on just that little bit longer
in the enchanted soil. If you're in Kyoto a day
or two out from sakura season, the Botanical
Gardens might just save the day.

Genko-an temple
源光庵

Secret northern temple with two impressive windows.

47 Takagamine Kitatakaminecho
Kita-ku

492 1858

Takagamine Genkoanmae

Mon–Sun 9am–5pm

JP¥
¥ ¥

W
genkouan.or.jp

A sense of peace seems to descend from the mountains over this less-travelled part of northern Kyoto, making a daytrip to Genko-an a special experience. The Second Abbot of Daitoku-ji temple, Tetsuo Giko, founded Genko-an in order to further the Soto Zen principals. The 'an' suffix denotes a house or shelter and Genko-an's main hall, built by Seika Koji in 1694, is more sedate and streamlined than a temple. Make sure to gaze westward before you enter. The Zen Buddhist temple ascribes to the Seto Soto sect that looks towards Gangamine (Hawks Peak) and Washigamine (Eagles Peak). Soto Zen master Manzen Senji is interred inside and people pray at his shrine for blessings of good fortune. Most people make the trek to Genko-an, however, to experience the famous Satori No Mado and Mayoi no Mado, the square window of delusion and the round window of enlightenment, respectively. Meditate before the square window and then head to the round window where you can sit cross-legged and contemplate the enlightening power of nature's beauty, especially in autumn.

Kinkaku-ji temple
金閣寺

Standout temple clad in gold leaf and reflected in a lake.

---

1 Kinkakujicho
Kita-ku

461 0013

Kinkaku-ji temple

Mon–Sun 9am–5pm

JP¥
¥¥

W

shokoku-ji.jp/kinkakuji

A golden pavilion shimmering in the lake below. Whispered stories of a fanatical monk setting it ablaze in 1950 (popularised in Mishima's novel *The Temple of the Golden Pavilion*). A Japanese Muromachi period (1336–1573) strolling garden with bonsai and Japanese pines on small islands. All of these things conspire to make Kinkaku-ji one of Kyoto's most visited sites. The beautiful pavilion, clad in gold leaf and gleaming in bright sun or winter light, is heaven for photographers. If you're lucky enough to be there when it's snowing, it's truly a sight to behold. When Shogun Yoshimitsu died, he left Kinkaku-ji to the Rinzai Buddhist sect. Small islands with tortured pines complete a memorable vista. In a city with 17 UNESCO World Heritage–listed Sites, Kinkaku-ji still manages to stand out. Note: bus 204 goes between Kinkaku-ji and Ginkaku-ji temples, so you can experience gold and silver all in the one day.

Picnics
ピクニック

A beautiful day, a delectable picnic and the sights of Kyoto – it doesn't get better.

W

kyotostation.com
daimaru.co.jp
takashimaya.co.jp/kyoto
goodnaturestation.com
rau-kyoto.com
wifeandhusband.jp
kyoto-yaoichi.co.jp
sizuya.co.jp

Majestic scenery and glorious food – there's no excuse not to have a picnic in one of Kyoto's many places of scenic beauty. Head to department store food halls, like **Isetan** at Kyoto Station (see p. 137), **Daimaru** and **Takashimaya** for a mouthwatering selection of take-out bento boxes and prepared meals and sweets. **Good Nature Station** has healthy pre-made meals and while you're there, make your picnic luxe with a dessert from **Rau** (see p. 88). **AWOMB Karasuma Honten** (see p. 56) makes a colourful and tasty picnic set and **Wife & Husband** (see p. 45), conveniently near the **Botanical Gardens** (see p. 176), make picnic hampers that include deck chairs and umbrellas. Head to **Natural Lawson** for vegan and organic choices (and delicious tamago/egg sandwiches with lashings of mayo). Try **Sizuya** for bready goodness and **Yaoichi** supermarket for bento boxes and fresh produce. The best places to picnic? The Botanical Gardens, Mount Hiei, Kibune, the Kamogawa Delta, Arashiyama by the Togetsu-kyo Bridge, Maruyama Park and Kyoto Gyoen National Garden.

Temples & gardens

MINDFUL EXPERIENCES

Kyoto has taught us how we would like to live in the world: cultivating a love of everyday beauty and an appreciation for nature and her seasons. It has taught us joy in the small things, like blossoms, leaves and snowflakes, and to appreciate wabi-sabi, the perfection in imperfection. Being mindful in contemporary Kyoto is about finding the essence of the ancient city, quietly walking through the grounds of centuries-old Zen temples like at Kennin-ji (see p. 187), Kodai-ji (see p. 190) and Daigo-ji (see p. 191), or contemplating blooms and groves in wondrous gardens like Ruriko-in (see p. 197).

Mindfulness takes in a range of ideas in Kyoto: wellness treatments, food, craft classes, spirituality and philosophy, as well as finding poetry in nature, like in the haiku at Rakushisha (see p. 196). It is practised in the tea ceremony, meditation, at onsen (hot springs) and during shinrin yoku (forest bathing). It can be found in learning and creativity, trying your hand at calligraphy, ikebana (the art of flower arranging), and in crafting ceramics and dyeing textiles, or fortifying your body with a vegetarian shojin ryori feast at Ajiro (see p. 185). Then, in keeping your travel experiences close to your heart, you can bring Kyoto mindfulness into your everyday life.

Myoshin-ji temple

妙心寺

A plethora of sub temples, lodgings, zazen meditation and a yin/yang garden.

1 Hanazonomyoshinjicho
Ukyo-ku

461 5226

Myoshinji

Fri–Wed 9am–4pm

JP¥
¥

W
myoshinji.or.jp

In the sleepy outskirts of Kyoto sits the Temple of the Excellent Mind, the self-proclaimed 'largest of all temples,' with around 46 sub-temples and countless standout buildings, many dating back over 400 years. The temple garden's azaleas were planted by famed Buddhist lecturer D. T. Suzuki; a 7th-century bell is on display; and the hatto (hall) features one of the Kyoto dragons, known for its central eye, which follows you around the room. Sub-temple Taizo-in features Michelle's favourite garden, overlooked by the Daikyuan teahouse. A vast, ancient weeping cherry tree spreads out before Inyou No Niwa, a unique yin/yang, dark/bright dry garden. Sub-temple Shunko-in offers accommodation at Tetsuryu-Kutsu. Book into their one-, two- or three-day meditation retreats (shunkoin.com). Popular zazen (sitting meditation) is taught in English in the magnificent prayer hall. Shunko-in is one of the rare Zen temples that perform same-sex marriages which includes the chanting of the heart sutra and the sake sharing ritual.

Ajiro
阿じろ

Seasonal shojin ryori banquet with a Michelin star.

28-3 Hanazonoteranomaecho
Ukyo-ku

463 0221

Hanazono

Mon–Tues & Thurs–Sat
11am–7pm

JP¥

¥¥¥

W

ajiro-s.co.jp

Kyoto's famous kaiseki ryori (refined multi-course cuisine) is a memorable feast for the eyes as much as the palate. For many however, shojin ryori, the Buddhist monks' cuisine, is every bit as impressive. Simple, vegan, or at the very least vegetarian and highlighting local and seasonal ingredients, shojin ryori on temple grounds is an unforgettable meal that, pardon the cliché, nourishes the body and the soul. Perched outside the south gate of Myoshin-ji temple complex (see p. 186), in an external annexe of sub-temple Shinko-in temple, is Ajiro, who has kept a Michelin Star longer than any other vegan restaurant in Kyoto. Upon entering, you will be ushered into a private room with wooden walls and tatami mats, where the air is scented with incense. When we went it was autumn, and the menu included delicate tofu, a light soup with mushrooms and yuba (tofu skin), tempura shiso leaves, kombu wrapped daikon, squash and chestnut soup. Booking ahead is a must. You can opt for the frugal lunch bento, but it would be remiss not to partake of the feast – a true Kyoto foodie experience.

Mindful experiences

Kennin-ji temple
建仁寺

Twin dragons reside in this extensive temple complex.

Kyoto's oldest Zen temple, Kennin-ji, stretches back to 1202 CE and is one of the Kyoto Gozan, the five most important Rinzai Zen temples in Japan. Easily accessed from Gion, the temple boasts many treasures, including painted screens by famed Rinpa artist Sotatsu, and Koizumi Jinsaku's impressive Twin Dragons which perch above you menacingly in the hatto (lecture hall). The temple features some deeply contemplative spaces: a sublime dry garden, the Garden of the Sound and Tide, and the Circle Triangle Square Garden (it is thought these shapes are all that are needed to make up the universe), both infused with mystical light. Further in, a mossy garden with maple trees becomes a colourful palette in autumn.

Kennin-ji also offers calligraphy classes and zazen (sitting meditation) under the instruction of Keinin Magame, the deputy head monk. Using the same methods as those taught to the temple monks (including the use of the Keisaku Zen stick, which uses posture and stability to bring body and mind into harmonious balance), this is a special Kyoto mindful practice experience.

📍	🚌	JP¥
584 Kumatsu-cho Higashiyama-ku	Gion-Shijo	¥
📞	🕐	W
561 0190	Mon–Sun 10am–5pm	kenninji.jp

Bishamon-do temple

毘沙門堂

An 8th-century temple, where falling autumn leaves blanket stone steps.

In the quiet outskirts of Kyoto, when autumn starts to fade, walk the gentle path to atmospheric Bishamon-do to see a carpet of fallen red leaves forming a crimson walkway on the stone steps leading up to the temple. The picturesque beauty of the vibrant colour is tinged with the deep melancholy of their falling, as the passing season gives way to the coming winter. Around a 20min walk from suburban Yamashina station, this temple has been dedicated to the worship of Bishamonten, one of the Four Heavenly Kings of Buddhism, since 703 CE (it was relocated to this site in 1195). The central Niomon gate overlooks 56 steep stone steps and frames the colours of the maples (and another red carpet of fallen leaves) beautifully. The temple also features an earlier example of the Kyoto dragons – Kanu Eishoku's ink dragon has eyes that follow you like a painting in a haunted house. Bishamon-do is also known as a spot for sakura (cherry blossom) viewing and features a famous 150-year-old cherry tree.

You can relax over tea and wagashi (Japanese sweets) at the rustic cafe on the grounds or take a picnic bento box and enjoy it while admiring the beautiful surrounding foliage. Hikers note, the forest path to Bishamon-do from Nanzen-ji temple (see p. 172) is one of Kyoto's best half- to one-day trails.

18 Anshuinariyamacho
Yamashina-ku

Yamashina

JP¥
¥

☏
581 0328

🕐
Mon–Sun 9am–4.30pm

W
bishamon.or.jp

Mindful experiences

Kodai-ji temple
高台寺

Temple with historic teahouses and a bamboo grove.

---

526 Shimogawaramachi
Higashiyama-ku

561 9966

Gion-Shijo

Mon–Sun 9am–5pm

JP¥
¥

W
kodaiji.com

While strolling calmly between the Yasaka shrine and Kiyomizudera temple, stop at Kodai-ji, a less-visited Rinzai sect Buddhist temple that dates back to 1606, built as a shrine to warlord Toyotomi Hideyoshi by his wife Nene. Both are interred on the grounds, which also feature a moon-viewing platform, a splendid tsukiyama (pond and strolling garden), beautiful canopied bridges and one of the best bamboo groves outside of Arashiyama (see p. 160). A rock garden is overlooked by a centuries-old weeping cherry and Kodai-ji is also a prime-viewing spot for both cherry blossoms and autumn maples, adding to its often-overlooked charms. Most impressive, however, are the original chashitsu (teahouses). The best known of these is Ihoan, one of Japan's only intact examples of a 16th-century teahouse, which impresses with its chunky thatched roof and large latticed windows. Tea Master Sen No Rikyo designed the teahouse in the wabi-cha style enhancing the chado (way of tea) of which Hideyoshi was a fervent practitioner. The temple grounds feature a variety of different tea ceremonies and tea experiences.

Daigo-ji temple

醍醐寺

Elegant temple complex with stunning architecture and gardens.

22 Daigohigashiojicho
Fushimi-ku

571 0002

Daigo

Fri–Wed 10am–5pm

JP¥
¥

W
daigoji.or.jp

Spreading out over the side of a mountain in south-east Kyoto, this sublime Buddhist Shingon sect temple compound offers a wealth of discovery for the ardent explorer. Around 40min by train from central Kyoto, it's perfect for a half or whole day of wandering. A UNESCO World Heritage Site, many buildings here hold great historical significance, like stunning Goju-no-to, a five-tiered pagoda often regarded as Kyoto's oldest building. Dating to 951 CE, it contains paintings made at the very birth of Japanese Esoteric Buddhism. The gnarled branches of spectacular weeping cherry trees can be found around the grounds, most notably near the Reihokan Museum, a great spot to visit in April. As significant as the blossoms are, Daigo-ji is also happy to proclaim itself an autumn garden. The temple grounds boast a stunning vista, a lake spanned by a vermillion bridge leading towards resplendent Bentendo Hall. Framed by fading gold, blazing reds and fiery yellows in November, the temple grounds are one of Kyoto's most scenic daytrips.

Chion-in temple
知恩院

Astounding temple complex with the largest wooden gate in Japan.

Although close to some of Kyoto's most popular areas, if you walk north of Yasaka shrine, you may discover that you have a precious piece of Kyoto almost all to yourself. Looming before you will be Chion-in's main gate, Japan's largest wooden gate, an ornate façade that beckons you into a vast temple complex. Steep stone steps lead you to the temple grounds where the chanting of monks floats on the breeze, bells gently toll and the ancient, intricately carved wood of halls and shrines sit in repose. The main temple hall is a must-visit during prayers – a solemn ceremony where a monk chants while striking various objects to achieve a literal spiritual resonance. The grounds feature 'seven wonders', including the Nightingale Hall, whose floorboards squeak to warn of intruders; the Forgotten Umbrella, reputably left behind by a grateful fox; and a picture of a cat that can see in three directions. Don't miss the temple's 70-tonne bell and bell tower, where you can strike various wooden and metal bells to release your own sacred vibrations into the ether. Chion-in also offers classes in calligraphy and meditation.

For a temple stay, head across the road to Wajun-Kaikan, Chion-in's contemporary shukubo (temple lodgings), which features a lovely communal bath and shojin ryori (vegetarian banquet) dinners.

📍	🚃	JP¥
400 Rinka-cho	Higashiyama	¥
Higashiyama-ku		
📞	🕤	W
531 2111	Mon–Sun 9am–4pm	chion-in.or.jp

Mindful experiences

Saiho-ji (Kokedera) temple
西芳寺（苔寺）

Over 100 types of velvety moss blanket the ground at this peaceful temple.

---

56 Matsuojingatanicho
Nishikyo-ku

391 3631

Matsuo-Taisha

By appointment only

JP¥

¥ ¥

W

saihoji-kokedera.com

Dating back to 1339 CE, Saiho-ji or, as it is affectionately known, Kokedera (moss temple), is a Rinzai Zen temple known for its lush moss garden. Some commitment is required to visit the temple; in an effort to keep the moss in pristine condition, visitors are limited. Pre-reserve two months in advance by sending an email or a downloadable postcard from the Saiho-ji website. On our allotted day we entered the temple grounds and followed the wonky path around the central lake, shaped like the Japanese character for heart (shin). Moss gathers around tree trunks and in between stepping stones, and it creeps over the island in the lake's centre, which features two connecting stone bridges that reflect in the mirror-still water. The garden is infused with a deep feeling of melancholy, its cushiony patina growing steadfastly over time, symbolising perseverance. Saiho-ji is a great reminder of how nature can be its own place of worship.

Somekobo Yumeyusai
(Arashiyama Yusai-tei)
嵐山 祐斎亭

Art reflects nature.

6 Sagakamenoocho,
Ukyo-ku

881 2331

Arashiyama

Fri–Wed 10am–5pm

JP¥
¥ ¥

W
yusai.kyoto

Arashiyama is a place of great reflection and the treasured villa of Yusai-Tei takes this literally. Once home to the master dyer Yumei Yusei, the villa itself dates back some 1200 years when the official court colour for dye was purple. It was replaced with korozen, a dye that changes colour and mood with the change of light. Yusai evolved this further at the villa, and his bold experiments can be seen in exhibits throughout. Take off your shoes and enter a series of rooms that show arresting views of Arashiyama's seasonal beauty. The iconic moment is a darkened room where five round windows show both the outside world and the reflected image on highly polished surfaces. Capturing striking autumn foliage, glistening snow or vibrant cherry blossoms, the old artist and his villa shows us how surrounding beauty can be harnessed and abstracted in textiles, tabletops and floors.

Mindful experiences

Rakushisha
落柿舎

Contemplative museum and garden at the former home of a famed haiku poet.

20 Hinomyojin-cho
Sakyo-ku

881 1953

Torokko Arashiyama station

Mon–Sun 9am–5pm

JP¥
¥

W
rakushisha.jp

Emerge from the north of Arashiyama's Sagano Bamboo Grove (see p. 160), with your head swimming with meditations and compositions, to find a tranquil area of rice fields and winding paths. Here resides the Hutof Fallen Persimmons, a museum dedicated to Mukai Kyorai, who once trained to be a samurai but chose the gentle art of haiku poetry instead, becoming one of Basho's main disciples. The clay walls and thickly thatched roof are a shrine of sorts, a pilgrimage where haiku devotees come to celebrate the life of Kyorai and pay homage to his works, which hang on the interior walls, inscribed in ink. Kyorai built this 'hut' when he went into seclusion at the tender age of 27. Kyorai's final resting place is here, as well as a persimmon tree that is said to be 300 years old, and part of the original garden (the hut was rebuilt in 1770 after being destroyed by fire). It is conceivable that Basho sat underneath the tree on one of his three visits to Rakushisha, and you can rest here too as you compose your own haiku, using Kyorai's and Basho's works, inscribed on stone in various places around the garden, as inspiration.

Ruriko-in temple
瑠璃光院

*A seasonal temple in the
northern mountains.*

5 5 Kamitakano, Higashiyama
Sakyo-ku

781 4001

Yase-Hieizanguchi

Mon–Sun 10am–4.30pm
(May–June & Oct–Nov,
reservations essential)

JP¥
¥ ¥

W
rurikoin.komyoji.com

Reverential silence blends with excited anticipation as you enter through the wooden gates of Ruriko-in, once a Meiji period (1868–1912) statesman's villa, now a serene temple hidden amongst the verdant forests at the base of Mount Hiei. Ask your accommodation to reserve a place for you as wandering the fairytale-like gardens will become a treasured memory. In autumn, fallen golden and crimson leaves scatter over small stone bridges which arch over burbling, koi-filled brooks. In spring, deep green moss accents the colours of the blossoming lapis lazuli. On the 2nd floor of the Shoin building you'll find the Yuka Momiji (floor maple), where a highly polished surface reflects and magnifies the surrounding foliage; it's hard to tell where the fiery colours of the autumn maples end and the polished surface of the table begins, as it all merges together in an utterly beautiful Impressionistic landscape. Explore the spectacular Mount Hiei location further by catching the cable car to the summit and taking in the arresting views of Kyoto, or trek across the mountain to Enryaku-ji temple (see p. 219).

Mindful experiences

文化と芸術

CULTURE & CREATIVITY

Kyoto's rich historical treasure trove of exquisite structures and objects fill otherworldly spaces and places, giving you a glimpse into how the art of constructing, making, shaping and designing runs in the very veins of the city and its people. It resides in ageing buildings and astounding monuments, and it's impossible to think of Kyoto without picturing the extraordinary temples and contemplating the rich thread of Zen, feudal and court culture that has shaped the city's cultural landscape.

The city's creativity is woven into the textiles and fabrics, and seen in the power of an inky brushstroke. It can be felt in the tactile grain of artisan paper, the smooth curves of carved wood or the rough-hewn texture of pottery – as seen at Kawai Kanjiro's House (see p. 207) and the Raku Museum (see p. 202). It can be heard in the plucked strings of a koto zither or the tip-tapping of geisha's geta (wooden sandals) on cobbled stones. Kyoto's feudal history comes to life at Nijo Castle (see p. 203), or when you walk through the retreat of the elite at the Old Mitsui Family Shimogamo Villa (see p. 209) and experience classic Brutalist architecture at the Rohm Theatre (see p. 208). A history of astonishing inventiveness and beauty means that many hidden gems are waiting to be explored as you uncover Kyoto's creative spaces.

Raku Museum

樂美術館

Minimal museum showcasing historic Kyoto pottery.

87–1 Aburahashizumecho
Kamigyo-ku

414 0304

Imadegawa

Tues–Sun 10am–4.30pm

JP¥
¥

W
raku-yaki.or.jp

The 16th-century tea master, Sen Rikyu's wabi-sabi (perfection in imperfection) aesthetic for the tea ceremony was a major influence on the early forms of raku pottery. The simple, unadorned tea bowls weren't smooth or polished but instead reflected a rural eclecticism by being misshaped and tactile. The Raku Museum, on a quiet suburban backstreet, expounds the raku philosophy in a series of ceramic pieces (some that date back centuries), perfectly curated and displayed in darkly lit rooms where light falls on each object, illuminating the deliberately imperfect surfaces. The current incarnation of the museum dates to 1855, and is a space that reflects the ceramic style – unfussy and yet emanating a mystical energy. Raku was based around a series of set rules: handmade ceramics with a distinct method of glazing and firing which is still practised today. A standout feature of Raku-yaki is the restriction to black or red glazes, creating a uniform presentation of elegant monotone ceramics. Rules are made to be broken however and colour seeps into the work.

Nijo Castle
二条城

Samurai decadence and ornamentation reign supreme at this opulent castle.

541 Nijojocho
Nakagyo-ku

841 0096

Nijojo-Mae

Mon–Sun 8.45am–4pm

JP¥

¥

W

nijo-jocastle.city.kyoto.lg.jp

Luxurious crafting, shoguns, ninja warriors and the drama of battle – Nijo Castle's history as an ostentatious feudal site has made it one of Kyoto's most-loved attractions. Built in 1603, the castle was the residence of the first Edo period (1603–1867) shogun, Tokugawa Iyeyasu and the feudal lord and his samurai spared no expense. Assault the castle from the east gate. The first defence is the ticket machine, then you can pass unchallenged through the ornate Karamon Gate and head into the Ninomaru Palace. The detailed carving on the gate and the striking wooden roof show an astounding level of craftsmanship. Inside, intricate wood carvings, gold leaf and paintings by artists from the Kano school give a lush materiality to the rooms. The 'nightingale floors' squeak when stepped on – an ancient version of the security alarm. On the grounds you'll find the ornamental Ninomaru Garden, which has rough-hewn rock, a mirror-calm central pond that reflects beautifully shaped trees, and a canopy of weeping plum and pines. The castle is made up of three circles of defence. Breach all three and award yourself a ninja gold star.

Culture & creativity

Kahitsukan, Kyoto Museum of Contemporary Art

何必館 · 京都現代美術館

Intimate art museum with a sun garden.

271 Gionmachi
Higashiyama-ku

525 1311

Gion-Shijo

Tues–Sun 10am–6pm

JP¥
¥ ¥

W
kahitsukan.or.jp

Opened in 1981, this small, privately owned contemporary art gallery is a peaceful sanctum on popular Gion-dori. Akenuki Atsushi, in collaboration with owner Yoshitomo Kakikawa, designed the gallery to extend beyond the traditional concept of an art space. The dark stone façade is softened by elaborate, detailed stair rails and warm wooden accents throughout the interior. It's how we would like our house to look and feel – intimate and dignified. On the 5th floor, the iconic image of the atmospheric 'sun garden' features a small moss and rock island sprouting an acer tree, which gloriously reaches up to the sky through a circular hole in the roof. Opposite is a tea ceremony room showing works by Kagaku Murakami. The five rooms show temporary art exhibits (photography, painting, sculpture and ceramics) and the basement houses a permanent collection of Rosanjin Kitaoji's colourful ceramics. Aficionados of publication design will find a series of exquisite, limited-edition books for sale.

Minamiza Kabuki Theatre
南座

*An arresting monument
to kabuki theatre.*

198 Nakanocho
Higashiyama-ku

561 1155

Gion-Shijo

Hours vary, check the website

JP¥

¥¥

W

shochiku.co.jp

As you cross Shijo bridge into Gion, you'll notice an ornate building façade commanding some serious real estate on the right side of the road. This monumental structure, with its gabled roof, kanji tablets and colourful theatrical illustrations, is the Minamiza. It's the main Kyoto destination for one of Japan's most famous arts: kabuki theatre, a beguiling performance featuring comedic and tragic elements, soap opera, musical theatre and farce, with a hefty dose of make-up and costumes that continue to inspire many of the great Western fashion houses. Minamiza was built in 1929 to house a theatre company thought to go back as far as 1610. The entrance hall is a sumptuous feast for the eyes and features spectacular hanging lanterns, and the performance space continues the ostentation – a vast room with a notable ceiling. Book in for a show but note: kabuki ticket prices can reflect the duration or opulence of the performance, so be sure to check first.

Culture & creativity

Nishijin Textile Center
西陣織会館

Faded glamour textile store with daily fashion shows and an informative museum.

Horikawa Imadegawa
Minami-iru
Kamigyo-ku

451 9231

Imadegawa

Tues–Sun 9am–5pm

JP¥

¥

W

nishijin.or.jp/eng/brochure

The Nishijin Textile Center is resolutely stuck in the '60s and so, having never left, it's come right back into fashion. A textile showroom with a definite *Mad Men* appeal, this authentic mid-century department store is the epitome of retro cool. At regular intervals throughout the day, the store presents a kimono parade, complete with chintzy Japanese stage settings and elevator music. Witness Japanese models in full make-up parading in beautiful kimonos to the muzak version of Nirvana's 'Smell's Like Teen Spirit' – it's great fun. Upstairs, the showroom sells quality furoshiki, tenugui, kimonos, obi sashes, silk ties and kokeshi dolls that all make perfect Kyoto omiyage (local souvenirs). The museum of looms and weaving accessories has regular weaving demonstrations that will bring you up to date on your straight and diagonal interlocking and jacquard patterns. If you want to get hands on, enrol in a loom weaving class. You can also hire a 12-layered kimono, traditionally worn by a geisha or maiko (apprentice geisha), have it fitted, then strut your splendid stuff around Kyoto for the day.

Kawai Kanjiro's House
河井寛次郎記念館

Treasured mingei (folk craft) movement ceramicist's house and studio.

569 Gojozaka Kaneuchicho
Higashiyama-ku

561 3585

Kyomizu-Gojo

Tues–Sun 10am–5pm

JP¥
¥ ¥

W
kanjiro.jp

Famed Showa period (1926–89) folk artist Kawai Kanjiro, one of the founding members of the mingei (folk craft) movement, lived and worked in this house which is now an inspiring museum. Kanjiro's purpose-built machiya (traditional wooden townhouse) is sacred ground where you will be taken from concept to completion in a series of rooms which display many of Kanjiro's works, some in glass cases, some placed in various tableaux about the spaces or exhibited as vases holding fresh flowers. Kanjiro experimented with glazes and firing techniques. He was modest (he refused to accept the offer of National Living Treasure), and his works, inspired by nature, reflect this. They keep to a colour palette of cobalt, deep red, copper and brown, which makes the collection cohesive and elegant. You'll eventually arrive outside to marvel at his impressive eight-chambered noborigama kiln 'Shokei,' where he fired his creations. You can shut your eyes and imagine the master at work.

Culture & creativity

The Rohm Theatre
ロームシアター京都

A brutalist gem remastered.

13 Rohm Theatre
Okazakisaishoji-cho
Kyoto Park Plaza, Sakyo-ku

754 0990

Higashiyama

Tues–Sun 8am–10pm

JP¥

¥

W

rohmtheatrekyoto.jp/en

Boasting neighbours such as the Heien shrine and the Kyoto Municipal Museum of Art, the Rohm Theatre has carved its own place in a landscape full of cultural history. Its temple-shaped roof perfectly reflects the Kyoto monuments in the surrounding hills, and the minimalist grey slate of the exterior now looks timeless instead of out of time. Designed by modernist architect Kunio Maekawa, it opened to much acclaim in 1960 but was neglected in later years. Its prime real estate and award-winning architecture was revered by the Rohm group who saved it from demolition, and a dedicated team led by Hisao Koyama, repaired and remastered this mid-century brutalist gem which reopened in 2016. Now architecture pilgrims trek to see the theatre in all its restored glory, especially its cavernous performance hall – an opulent spectacle. Savvy bookstore **Tsutaya** has also taken up residence here, further enhancing the building's cachet.

Old Mitsui Family Shimogamo Villa
旧三井家下鴨別邸

A superlative example of classical Japanese architecture in the villa retreat of a famous family.

58 2 Shimogamo Miyakawacho Sakyo-ku

366 4321

Demachiyanagi

Thurs–Tues 9am–5pm

JP¥

¥

W

kyoto.travel/en/historic-sites/258.html

Once home to members of the powerful Mitsui clan, this hidden villa is a Taisho period (1912–26) beauty that conjures up images of the simple opulence of the wealthy in Kyoto. Constructed in 1925, and refurbished and opened to the public in 2016, it sits at the very point of the Kamogawa Delta, hidden in the forests around benevolent Shimogamo shrine. Hachiroemon Takenime (the 10th head of the clan) built the villa for the extended Mitsui family to use as a peaceful and enchanting retreat. The family has since moved on, but you can stroll the gently haunted halls and feel just how perfect it must have been to have such an exquisite haven. The gabled roofing and intricate woodwork are an impressive sight seen from Sasaki Izuro's serene landscaped garden. Inside, light diffuses through shoji screens and warms tatami mats and wooden floorboards, and the sun's beams fall on the settled dust of history. Arrive early for lunch and tea sets in the modest tearoom, which regularly sell out, and gaze out onto a tranquil pond with artfully arranged stepping stones placed in a lush, mossy grove.

Culture & creativity

DAYTRIP
LAKE BIWA

琵琶湖

East of Kyoto, you'll find Lake Biwa, Japan's largest freshwater lake, and one of the world's most ancient (an estimated 4 million years old). You can easily make various daytrips to parts of the west and east, where you'll find some singular Kyoto experiences, including unique shrines, torii gates and temples, sacred islands, castles, abundant aquatic and avian life, beaches and quaint towns and villages.

The west side of Lake Biwa is easily reached on the JR Kosei line from Kyoto Station. Don't miss Mangetsu-ji's **Ukimido**, an atmospheric 'floating' temple – a spectacular sight at the end of a bridge that spans the waters of the lake on wooden stilts. Further along the line, fans of the 'floating gates' of Hakone and Miyajima will find the torii gate of **Shirahige shrine** is another great photo opportunity. Visit at sunset when the spectacular torii gate seemingly floats on the open water, illuminated for an atmospheric view as the darkness sets in.

The east side of Lake Biwa can be reached on the Biwako line from Kyoto Station. You'll find the ruins of **Azuchi castle** at **Omi Hachiman**, a beautiful canal town on the Nakasendo trail, also notable for the ancient **Himure Hachimangu shrine**. Head to nearby Azuchi station and get a taxi to stunning **Kyorinbo**, a recently rediscovered temple that dates back to 605 CE. Go in autumn, when you'll find the blazing colours of the leaves and vivid greens of the moss intensely memorable. Make sure to swing by **La Collina** for some delectable castella cake and where you can marvel at the oddball architecture, which features a fully grass thatched roof (which has to be tended to by gardeners). Further north, **Hikone Castle** is a designated National Treasure. Don't miss adjacent **Genkyu-en**, a 17th-century landscaped garden with ponds linked by islands and bridges. To the south-east of the lake is the **Miho Museum**. A long tunnel cuts through the mountains delivering you to I. M. Pei's monumental structure that houses the museum, a butterfly of metal and glass crouched in a secret forest haven. Inside is a superb collection of art and craft from ancient Japan, China, western and southern Asia, Egypt, Greece and Rome.

GETTING THERE

For the west side of the lake, take the JR Kosei or Sanjo Keihan line to Yamashina or the JR line towards Shiga. For the east side, take the Biwako line from Kyoto station towards Otsu. For the Miho Museum take the Rapid train from JR Kyoto to Ishihama station (15min), then the number 150 or 50 bus from stop number 3 (40min). Driving from Kyoto to the Miho Museum takes around one hour.

DAYTRIP
NARA
奈良

Nara is Japan's oldest capital, one of the country's most beloved regions (mostly for its free-roaming deer) and easily accessed by train from Kyoto. It's a town steeped in religious significance with a long history of artisan crafts, beautiful parks, ancient structures and premium food specialities.

Nara Park is a major tourist destination and for good reason. It was established in 1880 and has grown organically around some of Nara's main attractions. The free-roaming deer (certified National Treasures and thought of as the 'messengers of the gods'), are only too happy for you to feed them their favourite treat of senbei crackers, which you can purchase from various park vendors. You will find the fairytale cafe and eatery **Mizuya Chaya** deep in the woods of Nara Park. Further in, you'll find **Mount Kasuga Primeval Forest**, a haunting glade with a plethora of fascinating botanical and entomological finds.

Nara is also home to some of Japan's oldest and most important cultural buildings. Its standout landmark is **Todai-ji**, one of Japan's seven great temples and the world's largest wooden structure. The temple dates to the mid 700s and walking around it you can feel the weight of history and the depth of spirituality. Admire the towering wooden ceilings and Japan's largest bronze Buddha, flanked by a range of impressive warrior statues. **Kofuku-ji temple** has an ornate five-tiered pagoda, and **Kasuga Taisha shrine** features an impressive 3000 stone lanterns. Architecture buffs shouldn't miss the **Nara Hotel**, a Meiji period (1868–1912) marvel dating to 1909, and the Brutalist **Nara Prefectural Office**.

The streets are dotted with craft, homewares and food speciality stores. The history of Nara's craft is deep and intricate. Ceramics, wood and textiles were made here in ancient times and are now showcased in many shops run by young creatives who still use handmade methods like dyeing, weaving on the loom and wood carving. Food in Nara has been 'farm to table' and 'slow cooking' for centuries. Specialties include 'day-of-the-boar' mochi (grilled, sweet glutinous rice cakes that you can see being pounded with a mallet like old times while you walk the main street), organic lunch sets, narazuke (various pickles with a mild, sweet flavour) and somen noodle dishes.

GETTING THERE
From Kyoto Station take the JR Miyakoji Rapid train (45min) or the less regular Kintetsu Railway Limited Express (35min). Driving from Kyoto takes around 30 to 40min.

DAYTRIP
UJI
宇治

Fans of matcha should make Uji a priority. Though it is not far from Kyoto, you'll feel like you are a world away in Uji. Green tea fans shouldn't miss it, as Uji is known as the cultivator of the highest-quality green tea in Japan, and it's a peaceful, strollable town with a rich history and many memorable moments.

Uji's boasts a spectacular temple, **Byodo-in**. The vermillion structure features the famous Phoenix Hall, with its towering golden Buddha (its phoenix is on the back of the ¥10000 note). Don't miss the dark and moody museum which features celestial entities in the forms of birds and children perched on clouds floating in cabinets and on walls. Outside the shrine gates, head to the banks of Uji river to **Taiho-an** where you can participate in a traditional tea ceremony. Make a reservation and enjoy the ritual – town volunteers host an informative and atmospheric experience every hour. Fans of *The Tale of Genji* (written in about 1010 CE) will find a **statue of author Murasaki Shikibu**, sitting by Ujibashi bridge. Across the bridge you'll find a **museum** dedicated to the famous novel.

Once over the bridge, take a peaceful stroll along the river, stopping to peruse the wonderful ceramics at **Asahiyaki Shop and Gallery**, displaying a range of the famous Asahiyaki pottery, made in Uji for more than 400 years. A torii gate leads to **Ujigami Jinja**, which dates to an estimated 1060 CE and is said to be the oldest Shinto shrine in Japan. Beautiful grounds and a unique prayer hall encased in a wooden, cage-like framework, make this oft-overlooked spiritual enclave a must-visit. Nearby is **Fukujuen Ujicha Kobo**, a tea factory, museum and workshop that lets you grind and prepare your own tea.

By now you'll be hungry, so head back across the bridge to Omotesando-dori, where you'll find longstanding shops selling tea-related food and souvenirs. Try the matcha soft serve at **Masuda Tea Store** (and a green tea shochu if you want to float through the rest of the day). Visit amazing vintage tea store **Terashimaya Yahei Shoten** to marvel at old tea barrels and boxes, and the well-worn lamps hanging over the counter. Try cha dango (green tea doughball skewers) and buy some green tea curry mix from **Itoh Kyuemon Byodoin**. Those with a sweet tooth, head to wildly popular **Nakamura** or charming, historical **Tsujirihei Honten** for an extravagant green tea parfait.

GETTING THERE

The JR Nara line from Kyoto Station to Uji station takes 20min on the Rapid train. For a slightly different approach, or if you are travelling from the Gion area, catch the Keihan Uji line train to Chushojima, which takes around 15min (limited express). Get off here, then cross the platform and ride 15min to Uji station (Keihan line) to admire the amazing Brutalist architecture (not covered by the JR Pass). Uji is about a 40min drive from Kyoto.

Daytrip

DAYTRIP
A DAY IN THE NORTH
洛北での一日

A journey into the verdant north of Kyoto takes you out of the city and away from the tourists. Kurama and Kibune are mountain retreats that offer onsen bathing, temples and riverside walks. Ichijoji is a vibrant university town known for ramen and home to one of Kyoto's oldest temple complexes, Enryaku-ji. If you are heading north in autumn, the train goes through the 'maple leaf tunnel' – a mesmerising experience.

Catch the train north to Demachiyanagi station and head to **Coffee House Maki** for a morning breakfast set. Then return to the station and catch the Eizan line towards Kurama and Kibune (the other train detours to Mount Hiei). The train line is charming – it's basically the train set you had as a kid but grown up. The compact carriages rattle through small northern suburbs past stations, some manned by one person. Bypass Kibune – you'll walk there soon – and head instead to Kurama station at the end of the line, which is protected by the prodigiously nosed spirit king Tengu. Catch the **Mount Kurama Cable Railway**, then walk up the hundreds of lamp-lined steps to **Kurama-dera temple**. This historic temple of the Rinzai sect is unique in that it worships an esoteric being called Sonten. Pledge your allegiance while taking in stunning views of the surrounding mountains. From here, embark on a 1hr-long atmospheric, but somewhat strenuous, hike to Kibune (or catch the train one stop back to Kibune).

    Kibune is a town framed by forests, mountain streams, waterfalls and rocky outcrops. If you are there in the warmer months, you are in luck. Kibune features kawadoko dining, where platforms are put out across the water and you can feast with water rushing beneath you and waterfalls cascading nearby. You will also find the peaceful **Kibune shrine** here. Don't forget to take the time for a much-needed soak in **Kibune Onsen**, stopping to admire the waterwheel.

    Then, catch the train from Kibune station back to Demachiyanagi, stopping at the university town of Ichijoji to visit impressive **Enryaku-ji temple** founded in 788 CE, an expansive complex once home to warrior monks and now home to the famous 'marathon monks' (a thousand-day walking challenge over Mount Hiei's sacred sights means the monks walk the equivalent of circumventing the globe). Head into town after exploring the temple for a tasty ramen (Ichijoji is famous for it), and make sure you drop into what *The Guardian* described as one of the world's best bookstores, **Keibunsha**, to peruse their expertly curated selection.

GETTING THERE

Take the Eizan line train from Demachiyanagi station to Ichijoji, Kibune and Kurama. Taking the Eizan railway in the direction of Mount Hiei will deliver you to the base of the mountain, which is a prime Kyoto hiking spot with staggering views over the city's expanse. A popular Kyoto hiking trail begins at Shugakuin station and runs for nearly 1km across the summit of Mount Hiei before arriving at Enryaku-ji temple.

KYOTO ESSENTIALS

Kyoto is a smaller city than Tokyo or Osaka. It's serviced by private railways, JR trains and an excellent bus system and it's a great city to walk, ramble or cycle around.

GETTING TO AND FROM KYOTO

From Kansai Airport

Kansai Airport (or KIX) is south of central Osaka on a built island 80km from central Kyoto. Kyoto can be reached in 70min on the Hello Kitty (!) Haruka Limited Express train. If you have a JRail Pass, you can ride the kawaii (cute) train for free – it's our favourite way to travel into Kyoto. There is also a Limousine bus which takes around 100min with the option to drop you at nine different points around the city. A taxi ride is an extremely expensive option, however some companies offer ride share with a pay per passenger fare.

If you find yourself at Shin Osaka station, it takes only 15min to reach Kyoto by shinkansen (bullet train) or it's a 27min journey on the limited express 'Thunderbird'. From either Osaka or Shin Osaka stations, Kyoto is accessible in 30min on the JR Special Rapid Service for TSURUGA.

From Tokyo by Shinkansen (bullet train) if you have a JRail Pass

Japan's fast trains are a joy to ride, and so convenient; download the NAVITIME app for seamless connection info. From Tokyo or Shinagawa stations, it takes 2hr, 40min to Kyoto on the Hikari Shinkansen and around 2hr, 10min on the super-fast Nozomi Shinkansen. On a clear day Mount Fuji can be viewed from the right-hand side of the train. Make sure to grab a bento box for your journey and sit back and enjoy the ride.

Bag courier services

Carrying your bag to train stations or from airports can be anything from annoying to difficult. Ask your hotel to have your bags sent on to your next destination. Couriers usually deliver overnight, with a fixed price per size and piece of luggage. For us it is often the equivalent cost of getting a couple of taxis to and from our destination, and having no bags is liberating.

GETTING AROUND KYOTO

Subway

Kyoto's rail system is made up of a multitude of private rail lines (Subway, Hankyu, Keihan and Eizan lines to name a few). Each line has their own daily travel cards, so planning your day around travel on one of the private lines can be useful. You can buy an ICOCA, SUICA or PASMO smart card at station machines and load it up with money for use on most trains and buses. Or go digital by adding your card to your phone wallet. Tap on and off the readers at station gates; it's a breezy way to get around Kyoto. Having said that, sometimes it will work out cheaper if you get a one- or three-day pass if you are going to be using the trains a lot. IC cards can also be used at vending machines and often in shops or at coin lockers. Not enough money on your card? Don't worry you can adjust your fare at a fare-adjustment machine when you get to your destination. Your JRail Pass can get you from Kyoto Station to Arashiyama, or down to Uji (see p. 216) and Nara (see p. 214), so keep it with you.

Bus

Buses are a great way to get to temples and shrines that aren't accessible via the rail lines. There are two main bus lines – the regular bus service and Raku buses, which are set up for tourism and service most of the popular sights. Raku buses are numbered 100, 101 and 102. Board from the rear and pay into a machine at the front on exit. Pay using exact money. If you can't, there is a change machine beneath the payment slot that breaks down coins and ¥1000 notes. You can buy an all-day bus pass from convenience stores, the Kyoto Station Bus Information Centre, from bus drivers and at some hotels.

Walking

Walking is our favourite way to explore Kyoto. Make sure you get lost in the process of finding your destination while exploring one of the world's most beautiful cities. Pack your water bottle, head to the konbini (convenience stores) for some snacks and make a date with your trainers to walk Kyoto.

Bicycles

Bicycles are one of the best ways to get around in Kyoto. Both old-school bikes and electric bikes are available for hire around train stations, at D&Department (see p. 107) and TSite. There are so many great places to hire a bike, here are a few we love: J-Cycle (j-cycle.com); Cycle Kyoto (cyclekyoto.net); Fuune Rental Bicylce (fuune.jp/en) and our favourite Bruno Bike (brunobike.jp). You can hire a bike by the hour or for a flat daily fee. Some of the above also offer a 24hr flat fee. Make sure you check your hotel as they may offer a free bicycle service. Our favourite hotel Marufuku offers electric bike hire.

KYOTO ESSENTIALS

Taxi

Taxi ranks can be found outside most train stations, bus terminals and larger shops, but you can flag down taxis just about anywhere – just hold up your hand. Free taxis will have illuminated signs at night. During the day, check a sign in the corner of the front window. Free is 空車. Full is 賃走中. Saying a simple 'hello' when you enter helps (konnichiwa or the kansai hello 'maido'). If you have an address written in Japanese, the driver can put it into their satellite navigation. There is no need to tip, and most taxis take credit cards.

Google Maps

We don't need to tell you that this app will save your life while navigating Kyoto – Japanese address systems are complicated (see below) and Google Maps has become so sophisticated in recent years, you'll be able to meander your way to most destinations or find the nearest train station or restaurant. What a time to be alive!

Addresses

Being able to key an address into Google Maps has saved some of the difficulty travellers have had in the past navigating the Japanese address system. Kyoto addresses take it one step further and have their own complexities unique to the city. The city was laid out in a grid system in 794 CE and the system of address by grid is still used today. The address system essentially pulls apart the city from areas to neighbourhoods to the nearest intersection, then to the street and the land number.

Essentially all you need to know is the explanation below of this example address:

11-1 Murasakino Higashifujin-Omoricho, Kita-ku, Kyoto, 603-8223

The above address starts with 11-1. 11 is the 'area block', 1 is the land number (house or shop etc), on Murasakino Street, with Higashifujin-Omoricho being the nearest intersection. The address is located in the Kita Ward which is the area or suburb and known in Japanese as 'ku'; in this book you'll see us use the suffix of 'ku', not 'ward', in addresses. 603-8223 is the postcode. It does actually make a lot of sense once you get the hang of it ... we promise.

One thing to confuse travellers is the house numbers. The second house on a street may not be situated next to the third house; the second house could be next to the 30th house as they are numbered by when the houses were built on the street or in the area. Phew!

LIVE LIKE A LOCAL

Etiquette guide

Manners are very important in Japan and more so in an elegant city like Kyoto. Always be polite. Invoke your inner sense of calm and treat everyone with respect, and respect will be returned to you.

Kyoto Essentials

KYOTO ESSENTIALS

Lately, with the return of tourists to Kyoto on a large scale, following the Covid-19 pandemic, manners can be found lacking – people think that because they are on holiday they can act as they please. However, Kyoto is a refined city where displaying courtesy and observing consideration for others can get you a long way. So try it.

Slip-on shoes are your friend – you will often have to take off your shoes when entering buildings and put them on again when you leave. Remove your shoes before stepping on a tatami mat or entering a house. Many restaurants will also require you to remove your shoes, but the staff will let you know. There are usually slippers provided, but these are only for wearing to the bathroom. You should also take your shoes off when entering a clothing store change room.

Don't do any of the following things unless you want a disapproving stare from a local: blowing your nose in public (even sniffing is a bit 'on the nose'); not wearing a mask when you have a cold or feel unwell; eating and drinking while walking – find a quiet spot if you have nabbed some take-away from a konbini (convenience store); talking loudly – anywhere, especially on a train, and especially on your phone; taking a wet umbrella into a shop, instead use the bags or holders provided.

Queuing
Be prepared to queue in Kyoto, especially at popular eateries, temples and events. Observe how Japanese people queue, with patience and in an orderly line, not in a random cluster of bored people that make it impossible to tell where the queue ends or even if there is one.

Rubbish
You'll probably have to horde your rubbish as trash bins in Kyoto are few and far between. Convenience stores often have them and you'll sometimes find them at train stations and departments stores, but most of the time you'll be carrying rubbish around all day which you can eventually drop into the bin in your hotel room.

Konbini (convenience stores)
Dotted around the city going by brand names such as Family Mart and Lawson Station, konbini are open 24 hours and have all manner of convenient items for sale. Socks and underwear, umbrellas, skincare and sunscreen, and some of the greatest snacks and drinks you will ever come across. Kyoto konbini has specialist regional products like high-grade green tea drinks, wagashi (Japanese sweets) and tofu products.

Vending machines
Vending machines are everywhere, and the variety of drinks they have is staggering. They're incredibly convenient if you want a hot green tea or coffee in winter, or a cold drink

at any time of year. They can also sell anything from hamburgers to toilet paper, stationery, shirts, alcohol, oden, and cup noodles.

Money

Japan's currency is the yen, denoted by ¥. It comes in denominations of ¥1000, ¥2000, ¥5000, and ¥10,000 in notes, and ¥1, ¥5, ¥10, ¥50, ¥100 and ¥500 in coins. The ¥5 and ¥50 coins have holes in the middle of them.

There is a 10 per cent consumption tax in Japan. This is sometimes included in the listed price but often isn't, so check first. Sometimes a 'service charge' is added – for hotels and restaurants this can really stack up. Make sure you're aware of any additional costs before making a purchase.

Not all ATMs take international cards, so if you need to get cash, try a Seven Bank. You'll find Seven Banks in 7-Elevens and in separate outlets.

International ATMs can be found in some large stores and department stores, as well as at most post offices.

Shops and restaurants in Kyoto will often now accept credit cards, particularly since Covid-19, but many will have a cash-only policy – so be prepared. Cash machines (ATMs) at all 7-Elevens and post offices accept international credit cards.

Shopping tips

Many stores offer Tax Free purchases so be sure to carry your passport with you for proof of ID. Do not haggle in Kyoto unless you are at an open-air market.

Power plugs

Kyoto has great electronic gadgets and devices but remember that they are a different wattage (100V, 50/60Hz) to what you're used to at home, and the power plugs use different outlets (Plug type A or B). If you choose to buy something, you'll need to get it converted, or buy a transformer device.

Wi-fi

Starbucks and 7-Eleven stores with 7Spot have free wi-fi. There are free wi-fi hotspots on Shijo-dori. For your phone to find wi-fi hotspots, follow the steps on these websites (kyoto.travel/en/info/maps-apps or guidetokyoto.com/travel-info/wifi/kyoto-free-wifi-registration). Pocket wi-fi can be picked up at the airport or delivered to your hotel – check rates and order before you go. Try Pocket Wifi Japan (pocket-wifi-japan.com), Rental Wifi (rentalwifi.com), Japan Wireless (japan-wireless.com) or Japan Rail Pass (japan-rail-pass.com/services/pocket-wifi).

Prepaid mobile SIM card

Try b-Mobile (bmobile.ne.jp/english) for several plans with different data limits across five or seven days.

Check rates with your provider before you leave for Japan to see if they are competitive.

CULTURE

Geisha

In Kyoto geisha are only referred to as geiko (senior geisha) or maiko (apprentice geisha). The maiko are not allowed to wear wigs, so they are given elaborate hairstyles, which they must wear for the week and they sleep on special pillows to preserve the hairstyle. Maiko can wear red make-up and eyeliner; their inner collars are coloured and ornate and the soles of their geta (wooden sandals) are very high. Once they become geiko they can wear wigs and black eyeliner, their inner collars are usually white and the soles of their geta are much lower. If you're looking for a great primer on maiko before you travel, watch the gorgeous Netflix series *The Makanai: Cooking for the Maiko House.*

Temples and shrines

There are more than 17 World Heritage UNESCO Sites, temples and shrines in Kyoto, and this doesn't include some of the most spectacular ones, such as Nanzen-ji temple (see p. 172) or Fushimi Inari shrine. It's easy to get overwhelmed – there are so many things to see!

Shrines and temples usually belong to a specific sect or religion and can be very different from each other. For instance, Zen temples are peaceful, atmospheric and have muted colours. They usually have beautiful gardens with raked stones and moss. Shinto shrines are more vibrant, with vermillion torii gates and buildings. They often have food stalls lining the surrounding streets.

There are also mysterious breakaway sects and deities, which can be discovered in places like Kurama-dera and Tanukidani Fudoin.

LANGUAGE

Kansai language (dialect) or Kansai Ben

Thank you - *Maido ookini or ookini*
Hello - *Maido*
Please - *Okureyasu*
Welcome - *Oideyasu*
How much? - *Nambo*
So-So - *Bochi Bochi*

Pronunciation

Vowels are:
- 'a' (pronounced like the 'u' in up)
- 'i' (pronounced like the 'i' in imp)
- 'u' (pronounced as the 'oo' in book)
- 'e' (pronounced as the 'e' in egg)
- 'o' (pronounced as the 'o' in lock).

This doesn't change for any word. If two vowels are placed together, you say them as two separate, consecutive vowel sounds. Simple!

The letter 'r' is pronounced as a cross between an 'r' and an 'l'; the easiest way to make this sound is to touch the roof of your mouth with the tip of your tongue.

KYOTO ESSENTIALS

Useful kanji

Kyoto: 京都
Japan: 日本
Yen: 円
Male: 男
Female: 女

Entrance: 入口
Exit: 出口
North: 北
South: 南
East: 東
West: 西

Try to memorise the kanji for 'Kyoto', as it's especially useful for reading the weather on television. The kanji for 'male' and 'female' are also useful for reading toilet signage in some restaurants and cafes.

Phrase guide

Do you speak English? - *anata wa eigo o hanashimasu ka?*
I don't understand - *wakarimasen*
I don't understand Japanese - *Nihongo ga wakarimasen*
Hello - *konnichiwa*
Good morning - *ohayo gozaimasu*
Good night - *oyasuminasai*
Nice to meet you - *hajimemashite*
Please - *dozo* (usually used when offering rather than asking)
Thank you - *arigato gozaimasu*
Excuse me - *sumimasen*
How much is this? - *ikura desu ka?*
Cheers! - *kanpai!*
I would like a beer, please - *biiru o kudasai* (or add *nama* before *biiru* for a draft beer)
Delicious - *oishii*
Can I have the bill please? - *okaikei onegaishimasu?*
It was quite a feast! (for after eating a delicious meal) - *gochisousama deshita*
Taxi - *takushi*

FOOD & DRINKS

Food in Kyoto is very seasonal and has delicacies and flavours specific to the region. Shojin ryori, eaten by monks, is famous: small banquet courses of vegetables sourced from the mountains and served pickled, simmered or raw. They even use local 'bracken' in dishes. Other specialities are tofu, yuba (tofu skin), tea and noodles. Kaiseki ryori cuisine is a refined, multi-course banquet and can feature local chicken, beef and unagi (eel), as well as delicately simmered tofu and yuba and a variety of ornately carved vegetables. An elaborate kaiseki ryori feast can be expensive, but will be one of life's treasured memories. A tofu-based course meal in or near a Zen temple is also highly recommended. Tofu, yuba skin, pickles and many types of tempura and shojin ryori (vegetarian banquet) make Kyoto a vegans' and vegetarians' paradise, although it's always good to check for bonito flakes.

Kyoto has its own style of sushi. Mamezushi was developed for maiko (apprentice geisha) to eat, and is small, round and delicate. Regular Kyoto sushi is longer and more ornate and features a pungent mackerel on heavily vinegared rice.

Eating out tips

- Make sure you check the opening hours of your desired cafe or restaurant. Most cafes and bars shut for one day during the week, and many cafes open around 11am or 12pm.

Kyoto Essentials

- It can be good fun to try the omakase (chef's choice) at restaurants. This allows chefs to decide what they think is the best choice for you.
- If you don't speak Japanese, ask your hotel to make restaurant reservations on your behalf.
- Most places are licensed.
- Lunch is usually served between 11.30am and 2pm or 3pm. Set lunches are great value, especially at places that do an expensive dinner.
- When using chopsticks, don't stick them upright in a bowl of rice – this is a funeral custom. Also, don't pass food to another person or take food using chopsticks, and don't spear food with them (okay, we may have done this a few times ...). Lastly, don't use chopsticks to move a bowl towards you.
- It's good manners to pour other people's drinks as much as possible.
- Many small eateries have plastic food models out the front of their establishment, and many cafes have pictorial menus, which is very handy if you don't speak Japanese. You can take a staff member outside to the window display, or show them the menu and point to your preferred dish and say either version of 'please': 'onegaishimasu' (polite) or 'kudasai' (more casual).
- If you want to eat with the salary men and locals, there are many great, inexpensive options centred around or inside train stations.
- Make sure you try a kissaten. These retro coffee shops are a unique Japanese experience and Kyoto has some of the best.
- Tipping is not a thing in Kyoto. In fact, it will cause confusion.

Drinks

Sake is a big deal in Kyoto, so make sure you ask for sake specific to the region. It comes in sweet, dry and sparkling.

Craft beer is a serious business in Kyoto. Try Kyoto Brewing Co., Nishijin Ale Project (with added yuzu) and Ichijoji Beer Brewery who brew with the clear water from Mount Hiei. Check out Takashimaya and Isetan food halls for a full selection of drinks or your local konbini (convenience store).

HOLIDAYS & SEASONS

Public holidays

Christmas Day is a normal working day in Kyoto. You'll get all the commercial aspects of Christmas, including decorations and songs, but no baby Jesus. Christmas Eve is considered 'date night' in Japan, especially for the young, with couples going out to eat fried chicken!

New Year's Eve and New Year's Day are big holidays in Japan. New Year celebrations involve visits to temples to pray for good fortune and health in the coming year. Special wreaths called kadomatsu are hung on doors.

KYOTO ESSENTIALS

A tradition going back 400 years, kadomatsu are made up of bamboo and pine branches, and used to ward off evil. Many businesses close the week before New Year, and can stay shut for the first few weeks of January. Check any attractions before you visit to make sure they will be open.

Golden Week starts on 29 April, on Emperor Showa's birthday, and extends into the first week of May. If you travel around during this period, you'll need to book your accommodation and train seats well in advance.

Seasons

Cherry blossoms arrive in Kyoto anywhere from the last week of March until the first week of April. Blossoms typically last around a week.

Rainy season typically starts in the first week of June, making way for summer in the city which is ferocious and relentless in terms of heat and humidity.

Autumn foliage is sublime in Kyoto with leaves starting to turn in early November, peaking in the last week of November, and finally succumbing to winter in mid-December.

Crisp winter days with clear blue skies make for perfect woolly weather to tramp about sightseeing or cosying up in a cute cafe with a cup of matcha and zenzai (sweet soupy dessert). January can see some temples blanketed in snow, just when you thought Kyoto couldn't be more beautiful.

Festivals
Hatsumode (first shrine visit of the year)

Visiting the Inari Shrine at midnight on New Year's Eve is something you'll never forget but be prepared for crowds! Our favourite first shrine visit in Kyoto is Shimogamo shrine in Demachiyanagi.

Gion Matsuri

Gion Matsuri is Kyoto's biggest festival. It includes the folding screen festival, where you can visit many traditional houses. At times, the streets of downtown Kyoto are closed to traffic and taken over by all manner of food stalls. Girls dress in yukata (summer kimono) complete with purse and fan. It takes place on 17 July at the Yanaka shrine; celebrations last throughout July.

Gojozaka Pottery Festival

Pottery and craft lovers will adore this three-day pottery festival that takes place 7–10 August and showcases Kiyomizu yaki (Kyoto pottery) at around 400 stalls along Gojo-dori.

Gozan-no Okuribi (Daimonji)

Obon or Bon is a festival on 16 August that honours the spirits of ancestors. Kyoto's Obon festival is said to be the most famous in Japan. Giant kanji characters are set ablaze in the hills around Kyoto, guiding the spirits to the next world.

ACCOMMODATION

Kyoto has some of the most dreamy and authentic accommodation options in Japan. Why not try our low brow/high brow approach and stay a few nights somewhere comfortable that won't break the bank, then splurge on a life-altering experience.

Budget
Hotel Anteroom Kyoto, The Millennials Kyoto, Len Kyoto Kawaramachi

Well priced
Mitsui Garden Hotels, 22 PIECES, Omo by Hoshino Resorts

Stylish
Ace Hotel Kyoto, Miru Kyoto Gion, The Thousand Kyoto, Hotel Okura

Boutique
Marufukuro, Arashiyama house MAMA, Hotel Kanra Kyoto

Shukubo (temple lodging)
Myoshin-ji Shunko-in or Myoshin-ji, Daishin-in, Chion-in Wajun-Kaikan

Dreams are made of this
HOSHINOYA Kyoto, Hotel The Mitsui Kyoto, Muni Kyoto

Ryokan
A ryokan is a Japanese inn that can be up to 500 years old. The experience includes sleeping in a traditional Japanese room on a futon, and taking a hot springs bath, either in your room or in one of the gender-segregated baths within the ryokan (there can be both inside and outside baths). Each guest room is decorated in traditional Japanese style, with tatami floors and a central table.

A ryokan also provides one or two specially prepared meals each day, often breakfast and dinner (dinner can be served in your room in some establishments).

After dinner, your room will appear magically turned down with cosy futons and pillows.

The check-in hours and mealtimes are strict, and some ryokans have a curfew.

Some ryokans now have modern rooms too, if you prefer to sleep in a bed. Look around and find one that suits your needs. We always look for one with a private reservable bath, or splurge on one with a hot spring bath in the room.

The price of staying in a ryokan can seem expensive, but don't forget to factor the meals into the cost when finding a ryokan that suits your budget. Views and surrounding nature are usually memorable.

Staying at a ryokan is an unforgettable experience. We love to do it for birthdays, anniversaries and other special occasions.

Ryokans we recommend
Kikokuso, Togetsutei, Tawaraya, Hiiragiya Bekkan Annex, Kyoto Nanzenji Garden Ryokan Yachiyo, Ugenta

We recommend Japanese Guest Houses (japaneseguesthouses.com) for excellent ryokan advice.

ARIGATOU

A huge thank you to Hardie Grant Explore for their support in making this Curious Travel Guide, Hidden Pockets in Kyoto. *It's so important to us to publish guides encouraging detours and secrets that inspire a different kind of travel experience.*

Thank you to publisher Melissa Kayser for her guidance and making it all possible. Thanks to Amanda Louey for project managing, and being patient when bombarded with dozens of food images while we were travelling. Thank you to our editorial partner-in-crime Alice Barker whose nips and tucks and structural mastery help shape our wayward words. Big thanks to Megan Ellis for her always exemplary typesetting and Claire Johnston and Emily Maffei for their expert cartography.

Thank you to the wonderful Hiki and Ryo Komura for their translations and delightful company. Thank you to Coco and Makiko for fun times and teaching us the intricacies, quirks and sublime nature of Japanese daily living.

As always, thank you to our treasured friends and family who put up with 70 per cent of our conversation revolving around Japan and to Enid for the fluff and cuddles.

Shout out to Michael Khalil for designing us our own little Kyoto tsuboniwa.

Steve Wide and Michelle Mackintosh have been obsessed with Japan since their first visit over 20 years ago. Based in Melbourne, Australia, they now call Japan their 'home away from home', spending at least three months of the year there. Steve is a travel and pop-culture writer with a master's degree in creative writing. He has written 10 books on music genres and icons. He also hosts a long-running indie radio show on Melbourne's 3RRR FM and has interviewed and DJed with some of the indie scene's most influential bands. Michelle is an award-winning book designer and illustrator. She has also written four books: *Snail Mail, Care Packages, Sustainable Gifting* and *Pretend You're in Tokyo*. Her work has been exhibited in Tokyo, and she has a wrapping paper range sold in Japan. Together, Steve and Michelle have written, designed and illustrated nine books on Japan, which have been translated into multiple languages.

First edition published by Hardie Grant Travel in 2017 as Kyoto Pocket Precincts, where full acknowledgements for individual contributions appear.

This edition published in 2024 by Hardie Grant Explore, an imprint of Hardie Grant Publishing.

Hardie Grant Explore (Melbourne)
Wurundjeri Country
Building 1, 658 Church Street
Richmond, Victoria 3121

Hardie Grant Explore (Sydney)
Gadigal Country
Level 7, 45 Jones Street
Ultimo, NSW 2007

www.hardiegrant.com/au/explore

The maps in this publication incorporate data from OpenStreetMap www.openstreetmap.org/copyright

OpenStreetMap is open data, licensed under the Open Data Commons Open Database License (ODbL) by the OpenStreetMap Foundation (OSMF).

https://opendatacommons.org/licenses/odbl/1-0/

Any rights in individual contents of the database are licensed under the Database Contents License: https://opendatacommons.org/licenses/dbcl/1-0/

Data extracts via Geofabrik GmbH https://www.geofabrik.de

A catalogue record for this book is available from the National Library of Australia

Hardie Grant acknowledges the Traditional Owners of the Country on which we work, the Wurundjeri People of the Kulin Nation and the Gadigal People of the Eora Nation, and recognises their continuing connection to the land, waters and culture. We pay our respects to their Elders past and present.

Hidden Pockets in Kyoto
ISBN 9781741176988

10 9 8 7 6 5 4 3 2 1

Publisher
Melissa Kayser

Project editor
Amanda Louey

Editor
Alice Barker

Proofreader
Shawn Low

Cartographer
Claire Johnston

Design
Michelle Mackintosh

Typesetting
Megan Ellis

Production coordinator
Simone Wall

Colour reproduction by Megan Ellis and Splitting Image Colour Studio

Printed and bound in China by LEO Paper Products LTD.

FSC
www.fsc.org
MIX
Paper | Supporting responsible forestry
FSC® C020056

The paper this book is printed on is certified against the Forest Stewardship Council® Standards and other sources. FSC® promotes environmentally responsible, socially beneficial and economically viable management of the world's forests.